Teaching and Learning About Aging

by Richard O. Ulin

National Education Association
Washington, D.C.

Note

The opinions expressed in this publication should not be construed as representing the policy or position of the National Education Association. Materials published as part of the Developments in Classroom Instruction series are intended to be discussion documents for teachers who are concerned with specialized interests of the profession.

Library of Congress Cataloging in Publication Data
Ulin, Richard Otis.
    Teaching and learning about aging.

    (Developments in classroom instruction)
    Includes bibliographical references.
    1. Aging—Study and teaching—United States.
I. Title.   II. Series.
HQ1064.U5U48   1982   305.2'6'07   82-8312
ISBN 0-8106-1826-5

CONTENTS

The Author

Richard O. Ulin is Professor of Education at the University of Massachusetts at Amherst. During the 1980–81 academic year he was a visiting professor at the University of Denver, where he researched this book. He has also served as a Fulbright Professor of Education at the University of Botswana, Lesotho, and Swaziland. Dr. Ulin is the author of *Death and Dying Education*, published by NEA, and a contributor to many professional journals.

The Advisory Panel

Isabelle C. Chang, Librarian-Media Specialist, Shrewsbury Senior High School, Shrewsbury, Massachusetts

Janice Spinner Fitzgerald, Director of Public Relations, Cheyney State College, Pennsylvania

Rita Hodgkins, Librarian, Louis Pasteur School, Sacramento, California

John W. Myers, Assistant Professor and Director of the Clearinghouse for Elementary and Secondary Aging Education, Tennessee Technical University, Cookeville

Harry M. Peterson, Jr., Gifted Facilitator, Eisenhower Middle School, Topeka, Kansas

Marsha M. Resinol, physical education teacher, Canon McMillan Junior High School, Canonsburg, Pennsylvania

Jess Tabasa, Social Studies Chair, E. A. Hall Middle School, Watsonville, California

Preface

Between writing the first and second drafts of this book, my wife and I had a chance to go rafting down the Colorado River. It was our first experience of this kind—and far more rugged than we had anticipated. For two days, six of us novices and an experienced helmsman paddled furiously through standing waves and around rocks and hydraulics, taking turns falling in or out of the boat, though we usually managed to grab the lifeline as we lost our balance. The art of rafting, we discovered, is to "read the river" in advance, and at times we would even pull ashore and look ahead to plot our course.

Our guides had told us stories about Skull, most fearful of all the rapids we would meet, and also about the Room of Doom just beyond it. Many boats had crashed on Skull, and others had been sucked into the Room of Doom, where they swirled for hours, clutched in the grip of its powerful eddy. After carefully plotting its course, each boat shoved off into the rushing current. Each careened successfully around Skull and past the Room of Doom, but not one took the course its paddler had planned. The roaring river had a mind of its own, and our survival depended on accepting it and then paddling with all the skill and strength we had to ride it out.

Later, as I lay in my sleeping bag, restless in the hot desert night, I found myself intrigued by the correspondence between rafting and aging. When we go rafting, we spend much time planning and preparing; the quality of the trip depends a good deal on how well we plan and prepare. Much, however, depends on the unpredictable: on the weather and on the height and mood of the river. Much also depends on our ability, once under way, to "read the river," to sense its intent, and to improvise in accord with it. As we age we also find ourselves afloat in a current, forced to move with it and at the same time to manage within it. This book and teachers of aging work on the assumption that, as with rafting, one has some control over one's aging—not complete, but at least significant, control. It may be easier to teach someone to raft than to age; there is so much more to learn about aging. Events and experience, books and films and real life models, all can make good teachers. And so, too, can schools.

This book, it is hoped, will help teachers help some students understand more fully what it means to age, what it can mean to them, and what it has meant to others. Aging can be as thrilling and as frightening, as exhausting and as exhilarating, as self-directed and as unmanageable as rafting on a white-water river. Whatever teachers can do for students to make the prospect of aging less of a fearful nightmare, whatever they can do to help students appreciate the possibilities as well as the pitfalls of aging, may help students not only to relate more readily to the elderly around them but also to age with more grace and equanimity themselves.

To my home base, the University of Massachusetts (Amherst), I am grateful for a sabbatical semester during which I was able to collect my thoughts for this book. To the University of Denver I am thankful for an ideal place to collect them, for colleagues (particularly Jim Lawson), for a library, for an active Institute of Gerontology, and, not incidentally, for a swimming pool and the University's own ski hideout at Arapahoe. Thanks also go to Fran Pratt, Director of the Teaching and Learning About Aging (TLA) Project (Acton–Boxborough, Massachusetts), who encouraged me to undertake the work. Also to Sidelle Silverstein and Jean Bryant go thanks for caring as well as for typing. And to my resilient wife, Polly, go thanks for her stimulation and unflagging support during this book's dog days. I can only hope that my preoccupation with a book on aging and any distemper it may have produced in me have not aged her prematurely.

Richard O. Ulin

1.   Aging: What's the Fuss All About?

The tragedy of old age is not the fact that each of us must grow old
and die but that the process of doing so has been made unnecessari-
ly and at times excruciatingly painful, humiliating, debilitating and
isolating through insensitivity, ignorance and poverty.

Robert N. Butler

Suddenly, it seems, the elderly are news. Not good news, but news.
Old folks used to retire quietly and gracefully. But now, not always
by choice, they make headlines. Investigating reporters uncover scan-
dalous conditions in nursing homes. Congressional committees do the
same. Front-page stories report medicare and medicaid abuses
involving older people, physicians, and medical laboratories. Increasingly in the cities, older people become victims of violent crime, of
murder, rape, and robbery. Television news and documentaries regularly spotlight the plight of the elderly, particularly the elderly poor.
Is all of this merely a media hype? Probably not. This alone would not
account for the fact that stories, both positive and negative, about the
elderly are occupying a larger share of the news and of public attention.

Since 1960 three White House Conferences on Aging, each with
enormous fanfare and a multitude of ancillary meetings in towns and
cities across the country, have pinpointed the problems of the elderly
and have suggested possible remedies. Maggie Kuhn and her Gray
Panthers appear at Congressional hearings, form picket lines to
influence state legislatures, and, by making news, have a very definite
impact on the public consciousness. Recently, a spate of stories and
several TV documentaries have detailed the shaky financial under-
pinnings of the social security system; some even forecast its demise.
The results have been alarm among older people, a stir over legisla
tive remedies, and an alerting of the general public to its high stake in
whatever "aging problem" exists.

Other less dramatic events have also served to increase public
awareness. In recent years, senior centers, councils on aging, Meals on

Wheels, and other agencies for the elderly have spread across the country. They are both a result of this new awareness of the elderly and a cause of it. The very physical existence of these groups has brought senior citizens and their needs into the public eye. The Senior Surrey transports older people not only to the podiatrist but also to shopping centers, the hairdresser, concerts, and town meetings. As the public sees the senior center, the Meals on Wheels wagon, and the Surrey in operation, as they serve on town committees along with as well as for senior citizens, as they shop and attend sports events with them, the older segment of the population once again attains visibility. When, as now happens, thousands of low-income elderly serve in ACTION's Foster Grandparents program and each one becomes important in the lives of individual children and their families, old people come back into the national eye.

On the other hand, as the number of self-contained retirement communities, particularly in the sun belt states, grows, and as public housing units designed exclusively for the elderly proliferate, older people tend to be drawn out of the mainstream. But even these developments receive public scrutiny and require action by the wider population. Individually or collectively, the elderly may never gain as large a share of the limelight as that enjoyed by American youth, but there is no question that in recent years older people have become more visible and have captured more and more public attention. Their appearance on TV commercials—even if only to endorse denture adhesives and laxatives—as well as the continuing popularity of Hugh Downs' "Over Easy" television program, is additional evidence.

Perhaps nothing accounts more for the awakened interest in age than the sheer numbers of older people in the U.S. population today. In 1900 older Americans totaled only 3 million; thereafter the number grew phenomenally. By 1930 it had doubled, and by the year 2000 it is expected to reach 32 million. In 1978 over 24 million Americans—or one in every nine persons—had reached their 65th birthday. By the turn of the century it is expected that the fraction will increase to more than one in eight.[1] This "sudden" explosion will see the elderly proportion of the population rise from 4 to over 12 percent.[2]

No preparations were ever made for such a drastic change in the age distribution of our population; and although it should not have, the change has come as a surprise, leaving both the old and the non-old uncomfortable. A combination of factors accounts for this change: a tidal wave of pre-World War I immigration, a dramatic increase in the birthrate during the latter decades of the 19th and the early decades of the 20th centuries, and a sharp rise in life expectancy during the last 50 years. Not only have more people been surviving into old age, but also they are living longer. From 1900 to 1976 life expectancy leaped from 47 to 73 years, and today the fastest growing segment of our population is the over-75 group.

This is not the greening but the graying of America, and the graying has brought with it manifest challenges—not only to those who are doing the aging but also to their families and to the social order itself. As the elderly live longer, they have additional time to utilize, or at best occupy. They also must decide what old roles they can fulfill and what new ones they can assume. Women continue to marry men older than themselves and to live longer than men. As longevity increases, therefore, the imbalance between the sexes and the problems of widowhood promise to become even greater. There is also little evidence that urbanization, industrialization, and modernization are on the wane. Since these movements have historically relieved families of their responsibility for care of the elderly, it will be up to society to take up the slack somehow and to provide services (income, health, housing, etc.) for an elderly population of unprecedented size. The strains on our society resulting from competing demands by various age groups, particularly in times of inflation and economic decline, are bound to be severe.

Not only are the aged more numerous than ever before in history, but also they are different from all previous elderly cohorts. However unfavorably they may compare with today's younger generation, today's average over-65 cohort has more economic independence and is healthier, more vigorous, better educated, better informed, and more active than any previous over-65 cohort. These people, therefore, have greater expectations, are more demanding, and are also better able to make themselves heard, both individually and collectively.

Just how has the nation handled aging and the aged? Until recently we were a youthful people bent on pushing back one frontier or another, interested in innovation rather than conservation, in the future rather than the past or the present, in action rather than meditation. The country had never lost a war, its future was unlimited, its GNP would grow forever—i.e., we would enjoy perpetual youth. In recent years, however, the nation has experienced a sobering comeuppance. In a sense the closing down of our frontiers and the erosion of our political, economic, and military pre-eminence signal the end of national adolescence and of ebullient youth, and pave the way, hopefully, for a long period of ripe maturity rather than senes-cence.

A time such as this obviously calls for a reordering of values, a questioning of those that were heretofore held (many of which fixate on youth), and a reconsideration of those that cluster about age and that have heretofore been denigrated. With the nation–state in a peri-od of trying to make do with less and seeking a new role for itself among the family of nations, as well as with its own citizens, this would seem to be a most appropriate time to reevaluate the status and conditions of senior citizens who face a very similar situation. Given the temper of the times, the recently swollen ranks of these citizens, their capabilities, and the critical nature of many of their problems, it is small wonder that they, and others, are now kicking up a fuss. The wonder is that it has been so long in coming, and the pity is that it is only as loud as it is.

It is hoped that the new surge of interest in the elderly, and the closer look such interest entails, will result in a more realistic and reasoned approach to the aging process itself. It is in this change of approach that both the new science of gerontology and the newer field of aging education can play prime roles.

2. What Do the Young Know of Aging?

You don't grow old gradually, or on purpose, the way you go down-
town on a subway. It's more like finding yourself standing in the last
station wondering how you got there.

Cynthia Proper Seton

Why is it that whenever we go to a high school or college reunion,
we have aged so much less (i.e., better) than our classmates? An illusion, of course—but a very comforting and perhaps a necessary one, if
we are to enjoy what might otherwise be a very unsettling experience.
Each person (to some degree) is a victim of gerontophobia, horror of
aging, that afflicts society. Rather than accepting it for what it is,
preparing for it, and dealing with it rationally, we see aging as a
personal affront, an obscenity, an enemy, to be fought, rejected, or
denied. As a consequence, we view with distaste, devalue, and wish
out of sight and out of mind those among us who have already aged
and who remind us of our approaching destiny—first declining ability and then death.

We cannot fail to see older people among us who are losing, or have
already lost, their strength, their hearing, their sight, their agility,
their jobs, their family, their friends, and what both they and we
regard as their "good looks." For aging people not to grieve over such
losses would be unnatural, and for us not to be at least apprehensive
about a future that promises the same would be equally strange. Add
to the prospect of these losses one more concomitant of age: what to
most of us in the greatest loss of all—the loss of life itself—and it is
easy to understand why we abhor aging.

These things having been said, the questions still remain as to
whether the kinds of trauma suffered in aging and the special pain
inflicted on those who are already elderly are really necessary.
Despite the horror of nonbeing, the answer, I submit, is emphatically
NO. In other times and other places people have faced not only the
fact of aging but also the fact of death with greater equanimity than
we do now. They have respected and venerated, at times solely

because of their age, those who became old. Personal and societal values do not change easily. But with determined effort and in time, without radically altering our institutions, we can, I suggest, make America a place where children and adults are afraid neither to grow up nor to grow old.

Several segments of society will need to make contributions—old people themselves, the media, the legal and health professions, business, and government. But to parents and school personnel are given a special opportunity and a heavy responsibility. By precept as well as by example, they exercise a critical influence on the attitudes youth develop toward aging and the elderly. The critical nature of this impact derives from the fact that the attitudes children acquire in their early years tend to endure and solidify through later life.[1]

Educators, who cannot help but influence youth's approach to age and aging, would do well first to become aware of their own attitudes and preconceptions—attitudes and preconceptions that probably mirror those of the general population. As Simone de Beauvoir comments, the public's attitude toward the elderly has always been, at best, ambivalent.[2] Contemporary art, literature, theater, and popular culture have either neglected or denigrated old age, and most scholarly soundings of public attitudes confirm these negative views. In 1971 McTavish canvased the field and, on the strength of evidence in more than 300 research articles, concluded

> Stereotyped views of the elderly are prevalent and are uncovered in various studies. These include the views that old people are generally ill, tired, not sexually interested, mentally slower, forgetful and less able to learn things, grouchy, withdrawn, feeling sorry for themselves, less likely to participate in activities (except for religion), isolated in the least happy or fortunate time of life, unproductive and deficient in various combinations and with varying emphasis.[3]

Even professional health practitioners—doctors, nurses, and social workers—are not immune to the anti-age bias.[4] Psychiatrist Robert N. Butler and Myrna I. Lewis report that interns and residents commonly refer to old patients as "crocks," and whenever they can, doctors and nurses avoid working with older people.[5]

In 1953 Barron documented the fact that Americans stereotype the elderly and discriminate against them just as they do in the case of other minorities.[6] Nine years later, while acknowledging that the elderly do not fit the usual definition of a "minority" in that they have no distinctive language, culture, or history, Kogan and Shelton still conclude that

> While underlying sentiment may not be as extreme, we do feel that the dynamics of beliefs about the elderly are sufficiently similar to the ethnic prejudice case to warrant discussion in a minority group context.[7]

In 1969, Butler found prejudicial attitudes so rampant that he coined the now-popular term *ageism*, by which he meant a bias against the elderly and a revulsion to growing old.[8] A Harris poll sponsored by the National Council on Aging reconfirmed Butler's findings in 1975.[9]

How do we know, however, that we acquire these invidious attitudes when we are still young? Though some of it is conflicting, the overwhelming bulk of the evidence indicates that at least in America ageism begins early.[10] In one study Treybig finds that 3- to 5-year-olds "never want to become old."[11] When testing a broad sample of 180 preschool and elementary school children, Jantz finds that while they have little general knowledge of older people, they are positive only when they discuss older people affectively; they are negative when they describe older people in physical or behavioral terms and also when they discuss the aging process or their own old age.[12] Lorge, Tuckman, and Abrams agree that children look on aging negatively by the time they are 12 or 13.[13] Kastenbaum and Durkee find adolescents so preoccupied with the present and with themselves that they give no thought either to the elderly or to their own aging.[14]

Most studies also document the anti-age bias of college students. Kogan and Shelton's subjects express their distaste for the way the elderly look and say they would actually go out of their way to avoid direct contact with old people.[15] In a very different study, when Bell and Stanfield asked 280 college students whether they preferred to hear a lecture recorded by a speaker the researcher sometimes described as "25 years old" and sometimes as "65 years old," the response was overwhelmingly in favor of the "25-year-old."[16]

If we conclude, then, that the attitudes young people hold toward aging and the elderly are bad both for themselves and for the elderly, our next question is whether schools are in any way capable of taking corrective action. In Chapter 6 I suggest an answer when I describe a number of courses, units, and programs which at least purport to have successfully changed students' attitudes (and we have no grounds to dispute these claims). To my mind it is at least plausible that creatively designed courses, especially those that include an experiential component, taught by imaginative teachers can change attitudes—even attitudes as basic as those toward aging.

One caveat, however, I would offer at this point. Many educational institutions today are euphoric over the effects of experiential learning. From kindergarten through graduate school, teachers find students more and more restive in conventional classrooms. Many of them seem to have rediscovered Dewey, and in trying to fuse school and society, they encourage students to learn more by living and doing. At the same time, ironically, Propositions 2½ and 13 at the state level and supply side economics at the federal level tend to reduce education to "basics" by discouraging field trips and other "frills." However, experiential learning activities have been continued to some extent at all levels of education, and obviously many, perhaps most, of these activities are an improvement on conventional academic programs. But as was only to be expected, the movement has had its bandwagon effect, and some institutions, either to promote economic self-interest or to pander to student demands, provide not experiential learning but experience *in lieu of learning*.

If experiential school programs that bring students and old people face to face are to achieve their ends, they demand careful conceptualizing, clearcut objectives, regular monitoring, and, above all, careful evaluation. To assume that if one simply arranges for old and young persons to work or play together, they will then get to know and like each other is a bit of Rousseau-esque naiveté. Yet far too many educators rest content with this assumption.

In 1969, Amir concluded that intergroup contact actually can effect changes in ethnic relations.[17] However, he also found that these changes are not necessarily positive. The experiences even highly integrated Jews have had with anti-Semitism, as well as the bitter history of Blacks who for generations have lived in close but hostile proximity to Southern whites, seem to bear out Amir's contention. Not the mere fact of contact, but rather its quality would seem to determine if and how attitudes between groups change. When contact between the groups is forced or when it stimulates competition and tension, Amir found that attitudes actually become more negative. If attitudes are to change in a favorable direction, he found, the groups need to interact in a functionally important activity or in one during which the authority figure (a teacher?) displays a positive approach toward the minority group (the elderly?).

Auerbach and Levenson provide support for Amir's thesis in a vigorously controlled experiment with intergenerational learning.[18]

Without any prior comment, they included 26 elderly (65 and older) students with the 65 undergraduates in their introductory psychology class. They administered Kogan's *Old People Scales*[19] before and then after the course, and discovered that the attitudes of the two groups toward each other had actually deteriorated significantly. They attributed the deterioration to the fact that, at least in the eyes of the young, the older students clearly identified with the teachers (for example, by clustering around them after lectures), and also to the fact that the elderly students took only this one course, devoted an "inordinate" amount of time to it, and thus provided "unfair" competition. The act of merging the two groups without prior discussion and the highly competitive nature of the class, it would seem, determined that attitudes in this situation would not only change but also change in a negative direction.

Studies of this sort should, of course, be cautionary, but by the same token they demonstrate that attitudes toward aging and the elderly are not so fixed in the young, nor are they so much a product of extraschool influences as to make classroom efforts to change them futile. Obviously, these attitudes need changing, and it seems from the research, teachers can make a difference.

3. Can Aging Be Taught?

I hear and I forget. I see and I remember. I do and I understand.

Chinese proverb

Ridiculous questions, goes the old bromide, deserve ridiculous answers. And perhaps it is ridiculous to ask schools to teach children and adolescents what aging is all about. Isn't aging one of the few things all of us do constantly, whether we wish to or not, and without instruction? Even though extraordinary circumstances occasionally do surround aging, how can one anticipate the need for prior instruction?

Assuming, however, that some aspects of aging can profitably be taught to young people, one still may ask if schools are the best place to teach them. Given the heavy charges society already lays on schools, is it reasonable to add aging education to physical education, health education, sex education, consumer education, safety education, and driver's education, to name only a few recent curricular appendages? At a time when teachers are being warned to get "back to basics" and at the same time are being proselytized by single-issue advocates, by multicultural educators and international educators, by moral educators, and by sex educators, can they also be expected to work aging education into the curriculum?

Answers to the first set of questions, those that imply that any kind of aging education is superfluous, come from a variety of directions. First of all, to acknowledge that aging is inevitable is not to say we can do nothing about it: we can learn to recognize aging as a fact; then we can learn to understand its causes and its effects better, to adapt more positively to it, to cope with it better both in ourselves and in others, and to retard it—even to camouflage or deny it, if we do so fully aware of the consequences of our action. There is also a certain inevitability about the weather, and we can do little about it, but this does not stop us from discovering everything we can about it so we can act wisely or unwisely in light of our knowledge. Furthermore, individually as well as collectively as a society, we do have a major voice in determining not *whether* we are to age but what our aging is to be like. To age may be as natural as to breathe—that is, it may require little conscious thought—but individuals and societies, through choices they make, do determine how well or how badly they age, how they relate to old age in themselves and in others. However they learn it—in families, in peer groups, in schools, or via the media— children learn what aging and old age mean. Wherever they get it, this critical education will determine how they relate to their own parents and grandparents as well as how they act on questions of public policy that concern the elderly and how they feel about their own aging.

The second set of questions, those that deal with whether aging education should become a school responsibility, is harder to answer. One must acknowledge that in recent years we have put awesome burdens on the schools. In addition to satisfying our expectations that they teach basic cognitive skills and equip our children with an effective knowledge base, schools have had to respond to demands for affective education, vocational education, moral education, legal literacy, bilingual education, military education, peace education, drug education, etc. The list goes on. Each has had its persuasive rationale and its fervent adherents. Therefore, the possibility that some societal agency other than the school—perhaps the home, the church, voluntary associations, the peer group, or the media, or some combination thereof—might assume the responsibility should be explored.

One major reason, however, not to entrust aging education to any of these agencies is that none of them can be expected to reach more than a minority of youth. Also, as difficult as it is for the school to provide a balanced and comprehensive picture of aging and the elderly, it is even less likely that home, church, peer groups, or media will be inclined or able to do so. Nonetheless, if, as school people, we are really interested in changing societal attitudes toward aging, of course we cannot neglect home, church, voluntary associations, and the media. In fact, we should make every effort to enlist them in the cause of enlightened aging education.

In another sense schools have no choice in the matter. Aging education is already part of the curriculum and always has been. Students can't read literature or history without being exposed to models and issues of aging. When they study biology or psychology or family life, they can hardly avoid dealing with the nature and effects of aging. More important, the school itself represents a model of age-grading, defining as it does role expectations for students and staff in keeping with their age. School is one place students learn the prerogatives of age and its responsibilities.

19

The question, then, is not whether schools should teach about age but whether that teaching should simply happen or whether educators should give it forethought and structure. In this observer's view, the answer is clear. The American social order faces a kind of crisis in aging which requires that it call on the schools to take all deliberate action and with all deliberate speed.

In elementary schools the introduction of aging education need signal no diminution in reading, writing, arithmetic, science, or social studies. In these and other areas, well-informed teachers, perhaps with the help of elderly volunteers, can introduce materials and themes about aging that not only contribute to a subject's central objectives (e.g., critical thinking, scientific curiosity, empathetic reading) but at the same time develop healthy, enlightened attitudes toward age and aging. The same can be true in the high school. Courses in composition, literature, biology, history, politics, economics, and psychology—even courses in art, music, and physical and vocational education—can remain true to their disciplinary ends, and can achieve them just as expeditiously, through some form of aging education. Later I will suggest specific ways this may be done.

Many schools will find it congenial to leave aging to the established disciplines—for example, to have students in English do a literature or composition unit on "Old Age and Its Effects," history students one on "Growing Old in Other Times and Places," and biology students one on "What Makes the Body Wear Out." Other schools will prefer to make aging the multidisciplinary core of a course or unit, and then move out into the traditional disciplinary areas only as students see the need to look further into physiology, psychology, history, economics, or comparative cultures.

However schools decide to go about aging education—and there will be as many ways as there are schools—students stand to gain. First, they will learn about the objective world in which they live and mature and about an aging country in which old people already represent more than 10 percent of the population. They will learn why they and all humans age, what forms aging can take, what problems it can present, what control we do and do not have over it, and how we can prepare for its onset.

Second, in the course of acquiring a realistic view of age and aging, students may shed or avoid some of the stereotypical views Americans commonly hold about age and old folks. For example, they may learn that you actually can teach old dogs new tricks, that young fools may be at least as foolish as old fools, and that some people over 30 can be trusted. Contrary to conventional "wisdom," they will learn that—

- old people are *not* all alike.
- old people vary more widely than those in any other age group.
- older people can and do learn, but in a different way.
- most retired people do not move to the sun belt.
- older people are both capable of and interested in sex.
- senility is most *unusual* in old age.
- older workers have better attendance records and fewer accidents than younger workers.
- most older people prefer to live independently.
- they fear death *less* than do younger people.
- they do *not* become more conservative in their later years.
- they remain interested in civic affairs and vote with greater regularity than any other age segment of our population.
- to be old is not necessarily to be sick or infirm.
- intelligence does *not* decrease as one ages, at least not until the final moments of life.
- most elderly people do *not* live lonely, isolated lives.
- only a small minority of them live in institutions.

These are some of the facts of aging today in America that students can and should learn because they belie a popular mythology that exerts extremely unhealthy effects on our young and not so young. If it were to serve no other purpose, the capacity of aging education to dispel, or at least deflate, this mythology would earn it a place in the schools.

Other reasons, however, also readily offer themselves. For one, young people, who are themselves in the throes of rapid growth, have a built-in interest in aging. They need, of course, to understand as best they can the developmental stages through which they are currently moving, but to do so, they also need a perspective that comes only from understanding the total lifespan, what Rosenfeld labels "The New LSD: Life-Span Development."[1]

Part of that lifespan is old age, and any well-designed curriculum on aging will provide for its inclusion. Only by having some awareness of the tasks they will meet at each of life's successive developmental stages will young people be able to judge how they are coping with the tasks they now face. One fundamental aim of education, and of life, is understanding oneself, and part of that problem is that we are always in motion, always changing and growing. Aging education, particularly if it reflects a lifespan development approach, may help young people understand some of the puzzling, and often disturbing, aspects of their own physical and psychosocial growth.

Another, perhaps paradoxical, boon of aging education is that young people are given a positive future orientation. "If the future is to be really accepted," says Margaret Mead, "it must be anchored in a feeling for the past." Recent years, according to Mead, have given us "an increasingly present-bound generation," one that refuses to deal with history at all and lives in "a kind of timeless present." She charges today's youth with being

> . . . a generation who assume that the world is somehow finished, although possibly finished wrong. The same lack of belief in real change can be found in the doomsday approach of those who reject our present life on an endangered planet. Living in a world in which there is no one to represent the possibility of change, or even the conditions of the past, they find themselves unable to believe in the future.[2]

Mead appeals for a societal reorganization that would enable children to live in multigenerational communities where, close to old people, they would have constant exposure to the past and to change. Until, if ever, such reorganization takes place, schools can help fill the void Mead describes by introducing age and the elderly to the classroom. They can do so not only in conventional academic ways but also by bringing old and young people face to face in and out of school. (See Chapter 7 for a discussion of intergenerational activities.) Good aging education can help youngsters to a full awareness that Grandpa was not always old and bent; that time does pass, sometimes all too swiftly; that they themselves will not always be young and supple; that just as today Grandma lives in a world that is worlds apart from the one she lived in as a child, so, too, the world of their own adult and later years will be a very different place from the one they now know. Teachers and parents both know how difficult it is to interest young people in the past, in what they regard as "ancient history." They also find it ironic that young people who dote on *Star Wars* are unwilling or unable to make plans for next year or next month or even next week. If teachers and parents could see aging education as helping, even remotely, to make children *future-* rather than present-conscious, they would rally to it.

Not only can aging education provide young people with a sense of the past and a view to the future, but also if it stimulates old–young interaction, it may have a profound social impact. Young people can learn something of the past from those who have actually lived it, and old people will gain listeners and acquire a productive social role and a new sense of self-worth. In the process, those natural bonds between the quite young and the quite old will assume new strength, and at least one step will have been taken to keep our fragile social order from disintegrating along age lines.

If aging education holds a promise of helping our warring generations relate to one another more empathetically and amicably, this alone would justify its inclusion in the curriculum. Parents, teachers, and school board members, all of them either old now or about to be old, would do well to advocate aging education, if only on the grounds of self-interest. Human development specialist Jean Grambs reminds teachers:

> If you and I are to be secure in our old age, with pensions that one can live on, then youngsters now in our classes will have to tax themselves at a much higher rate than now. . . . Will they graciously acquiesce to the burden of paying for our declining years? Or will they refuse and commit many of us to an old age of limited resources and deprivation? The answer lies in how we educate these future citizens now.[3]

Pragmatic as well as theoretical, the grounds for aging education in the schools, it would seem, are many and strong. But none of them obtains if aging education turns out to be dull and fails to grab students. Nothing yet, however, suggests that this need be the case. In fact, what firsthand evidence this writer has indicates that at all school levels young people can be and are interested in aging as a subject. Scattered accounts of courses and units taught on aging detail unusual, often glowing, success stories. These reports, it is true, generally come from the teachers themselves. Since most of us are disinclined to publicize our failures and likely to exaggerate our successes, it is hard to weigh the evidence. It is also probably the case, as with any subject matter that is new and taught by eager volunteers, that until now aging education has profited from the Hawthorne effect. Most aging educators this writer knows are people with a mission, people who have a sense of themselves as pioneers and who teach with above-average zeal. Because of this process of teacher self-selection, aging education has enjoyed, in both its conception and its execution, a quality of instruction shared by few other subject areas. When and if aging becomes a fixture in the curriculum, the level of excitement it will then create remains to be seen. At this juncture, therefore, with what little evidence we have, all we can safely say is that, when taught at precollege levels by enthusiastic teachers, aging has proved to be an appealing subject to students, and that at least under these experimental conditions aging education appears capable of meeting the objectives its advocates have set for it.

4.   Are the Schools Too Busy?

An education is the next best thing to a pushy mother.

Charles Schulz

If we really need instruction in how to grow old, how does aging education get started? If schools actually are places where students can profit from exposure to information about aging, how, when, and in what form should it come? How discrete and how recognizable should aging education be? What is to be gained, or perhaps lost, by trying to infiltrate already established components of the conventional elementary, middle, and secondary school curriculums? If we are to have aging education, are teachers the only or the best source of instruction? If so, how much and what kind of training or retraining will they need? Can the projected outcomes of aging education be both cognitive and affective, behavioral as well as intellectual? Can opposition be expected and, if so, from whom? How costly will aging education be? These are only some of the questions that anyone interested in including aging education in the curriculum may well ask.

Here and in later chapters we will deal with all of these questions, in both general and specific terms. From our discussion of them, teachers should be in a better position to judge whether a school situation calls for some kind of aging education and, if so, what kind; to find accounts of previous school efforts aimed in similar directions; and to determine the best course of action.

First, the question whether students in a given situation need aging education is already answered by the evidence, some of it cited in this book, of America's growing inability to deal with its "aging problem," of our inability to handle our own aging, as well as that of others, and to cope with aging and the aged in either personal or societal terms. Those who find the evidence unconvincing or too wide-ranging may survey their own communities to determine how residents feel about growing old, how they relate to and feel about the elderly, what they know about growing old in this and other places and in these and other times, and what preparations they have made for their own later years. Using already tested instruments or devising others local-

24

ly, similar assessments of the knowledge and attitudes of students may be made at each of several grade levels.

The data from surveys such as these, along with the considered judgments of interested school staff and townspeople, can provide a starting point for building an aging curriculum. This information provides clues as to what students know, what kinds of stereotypes and misinformation they have already acquired, what experiences they have had with the elderly, what their attitudes toward aging are, and how, if at all, these attitudes change as they grow older.

With this information in hand, a school- or townwide committee can formulate broad objectives for an aging program. It can then decide which objectives are more appropriately addressed within the schools, which are more properly the responsibility of extraschool agencies, and which fall within the province of both and call for coordinated action. At this point the school/town committee might reconstitute itself (while adding others) into two separate committees, one of school personnel to formulate and implement curriculums and the other to devise out-of-school education and community action. The latter calls for work with, among others, the scouts, civic and social clubs, veterans' clubs, churches, libraries, newspapers, business and professional associations, police and fire department employees, and town officials.

If formed, a school curriculum committee must deal with most of the questions with which this chapter opened. Some it will be able to answer with precision. In the case of others it will have to rely on a consensus of impressionistic judgments. To wait for definitive answers to questions as difficult as these would preclude any program's ever getting off the ground. Indeed, as a practical matter even the formation of such a systemwide committee and the use of such a comprehensive approach at the outset are open to question. In some, perhaps most, situations the spadework for systemwide curriculum plans may more effectively be done by individual teacher probes, by aging units and courses initiated by a few dedicated teachers in a few enterprising schools. What is more likely to happen is that teachers of these units and courses will draw attention to themselves, prompt the creation of a systemwide committee on aging, and facilitate the committee's work.

Fortunately the field of precollegiate aging education is still so young that prepackaged schoolwide curriculums are not yet readily available; schools and teachers must rely on their own resources, without the temptation simply to adopt what others proudly claim to have worked up for them. Most school systems find that a "bottom-up"

25

approach to curriculum building works more effectively than a "top-down" one. Thus, even when a system places responsibility for its aging education on a central committee, chances are that teachers at all grade levels and in various subject areas will be called upon to prepare curriculum materials they feel appropriate for their students. Some teachers will be more enthusiastic, energetic, and productive than others, and some materials will prove to be more imaginative and promising than others. Therefore, like many of the questions posed at the outset of this chapter, the questions as to the level and the subject areas in which aging should be taught are likely to be answered on highly pragmatic grounds. Aging, in fact, will be taught wherever the interest is.

Two *a priori* questions, however, need be raised here: First, should aging education be consciously and deliberately inserted at particular grade levels and in particular subject areas, or should it unobtrusively permeate the entire K–12 curriculum? Those who favor the first approach fear that whatever becomes everyone's job turns out to be no one's. However, aging educators—if we dare use that ambiguous term—who take the second approach point to the danger of isolating the problems and experience of aging from life's developmental sequence and of removing them from ordinary curricular contexts. To do so at the precollege level, they argue, is to distort them.

Generally speaking, the elementary curriculum enjoys a flexibility unknown in departmentalized middle and secondary schools and can, therefore, more easily accommodate discrete units on aging. Elementary school faculty worry less about matters of departmental territorial integrity. They are relatively unconcerned whether an aging unit is more properly categorized as social studies, science, health, or language arts, and they are more comfortable with allowing a unit on aging to remain freestanding.

At the middle and secondary school levels, in a school that operates a modular or a mini-course program, teachers of any discipline may offer a module or course on aging. If no such program is available, aging instruction then must fall under the aegis of one, or perhaps more than one, department. When a school is large and progressive enough to offer electives, it may have the luxury of providing one or more courses in age-related education without altering any of the traditional departmental courses. English, social studies, science, and home economics each may offer an age-related elective which serves to meet the department's own individual objectives.

In recent years, however, the trend toward mini-courses and electives seems to have crested and declined. If secondary schools today plan to add aging education to a curriculum that is always perceived as overcrowded, most of them will have to persuade teachers that including an age-related segment or theme can actually expedite the achievement of a discipline's traditional objectives and at the same time provide students with a new and highly meaningful learning experience. Just as elementary students can learn to add, to listen, to reason, to write, and to relate to others through an age-related learning experience, so, too, can secondary students learn some of the skills that English, biology, mathematics, social studies, and home economics teachers are expected to teach, only via age-related units of study. In today's "back-to-basics" atmosphere not only the general public and school boards but also all concerned teachers, students, administrators, and parents should recognize that instruction in "the basics" can be enhanced rather than diminished by inclusion of an area with the universal relevance of aging.

Just as it is never too early to provide school experiences in art, language, science, mathematics, or sex education, so, too, is it never too early to introduce aging education. This is not to take Bruner's dictum simplistically: to assume that children at any age are ready for any concept as long as it is phrased in language they understand. To do so would be to suggest that a watered-down college course in social gerontology is suitable for high school students, and that by the same token, elementary students can profit from college and high school units translated into terms understandable to them. Nothing could be further from the truth. At each successive school level, students are ready to acquire more sophisticated concepts and to learn from different experiences. And the sequence is not invariable from student to student or from community to community. Thus, those who would establish an aging curriculum must make decisions in terms of particular circumstances and particular students.

The second question that needs to be addressed at the outset is the degree to which aging education should aim to achieve cognitive or affective ends. This is not an easy question, but some of the difficulty, I suggest, lies in the artificial dichotomy that educators often draw between the two modes. How can one predict when the acquisition of information will remain a purely intellectual matter and when it will produce fallout in the form of feelings, attitudes, and consequent behavior. School people and communities vary widely in the degree to which they feel schools should stress intellective as opposed to attitudinal ends, and their relative commitment to one or the other will be, and certainly should be, reflected in any program they initiate.

When school programs stress the acquisition of information and the processing of it, students acquire a body of data and learn to make meaning of it. In studying aging, they inquire into the reasons humans age, how they have aged in the past and are likely to age in the future, how people now react to and prepare for their own aging, how they respond to the aging of those close to them as well as those distant from them, what experiences determine these responses, and how people in different times and different places see aging and old age. In a cognitively oriented course questions of value are dealt with only when they arise, and then only incidentally and peripherally. A teacher certainly makes no attempt to implant "right attitudes." In such a program one finds little "experiential learning" and few efforts to create a mind-set, to alter attitudes, or to change behavior. Students are unlikely to spend their time in role play, simulations, visits to nursing homes, or intergenerational activities.

On the other hand, if the major objectives of an aging program are affective, if attitudinal and behavioral changes are emphasized along with, or more than, informational gain and cognitive skills, then the program may well stress experiential activities. Students may acquire knowledge about how and why people age and react to aging, but that knowledge is intended to serve as a means rather than an end, to influence the way students feel about and then act in matters of their own and others' aging. This kind of course usually posits certain values as "humane" and certain attitudes as "right," and deliberately fosters their acquisition: these might include an "acceptance of aging," "respect for age," and the "responsibility of youth toward age." Some curriculum designers and teachers may take a "value-free" stance, confident that "humane" values and "right" attitudes will prevail; the odds are, however, that despite the best of intent, their values will show in their approach as well as in their selection of materials and learning experiences. Courses that aim at having an impact on students' values and behavior are likely to feature experiential learning, to include role playing and simulation in class, and to stress face-to-face intergenerational activities with the elderly (e.g., to have students visit nursing homes, take oral histories, and intern in senior centers and other community agencies).

Each teacher, school, and community will have to determine for itself what its aims and its special needs are and to shape its aging program accordingly. However, while taking into account the individuality of their own situation, local curriculum developers should appreciate the fact that there are commonalities among students, schools, and communities, and that there are advantages to be gained if one examines precedents. To this end, we will outline some of the more successful efforts made in the field of aging education.

5. Aging: What Is There To Learn and Teach?

Sir, it is no matter what you teach them first, any more than what leg you shall put into your breeches first. Sir, you may stand disputing which is best to put in first, but in the meantime your breech is bare. Sir, while you are considering which of two things you should teach your child first, another boy has learnt them both.

Samuel Johnson

What should you know about aging before you try to teach the subject? It all depends: on what you want your students to learn, on who your students are and what kinds of lives they've lived, and on the particular school context—course and grade level and total curriculum—into which you want your teaching to fit. It also depends on just how much chutzpah you have, how much ahead of your students you feel you need be.

There are obvious benefits, of course, to you and your students if you can play the role of a learner. I would suggest, however, that you not plan to lean too long or too heavily on this particular kind of parity. Ordinarily you start with at least one advantage: being older than they are. In one sense you already know more about aging than they do. But you are probably well advised to make yourself considerably more advantaged. Whatever knowledge you can acquire of the history, biology, literature, psychology, and/or sociology of aging will contribute to your sense of ease with the subject and can facilitate student learning.

Your students will all begin at different levels and each will proceed at her or his own pace. The fact that you as a teacher begin from a relatively knowledgeable baseline in no way disqualifies you from joining them as a learner. As a field of study, aging is still in its infancy, and it necessarily borrows from a wide variety of disciplines. As a result, the "unknowns" outnumber the "knowns" more so than in established subject areas, and investigations in the field of aging profit by the collaboration of people with all degrees of expertise.

29

The kind of preparation you will find useful obviously depends on whether you plan to teach a course or a unit focused explicitly on aging, or whether you aim simply to enhance what you are already teaching—English or social studies or second grade—by including a dimension on aging. In the first case, along with some general knowledge about aging, you will want to ground yourself with specific knowledge in at least one area of aging (e.g., the biology or history or psychology of aging), a subsection of one of these areas, or some combination of them. In the second case, your needs will probably be better served by a broad general exposure to social gerontology, either through your own readings or through an introductory course. In either situation, if you have not yet been directly and significantly involved with older people, you should acquire some firsthand familiarity with them and with their day-to-day activities. To complement your academic background and to help authenticate your teaching, you might attend or teach at an elderhostel or work at a senior center, nursing home, hospital, or hospice. You might even join the Gray Panthers. These are activities, of course, that not only teachers but also any civic-minded citizen should consider.

Aging is as yet an amorphous and relatively unmapped area of instruction, but several large subsections of the field have now begun to emerge. These provide a variety of perspectives as well as a helpful entrée into the field for the newcomer. In the meantime, wherever teachers set their pedagogical sights on aging, they are likely to find comprehensible and helpful material in any of the various gerontological subsections. What follows in this chapter is my own map of the area of aging—highly arbitrary but hopefully helpful to teachers who are interested in what can be taught about aging and who are looking for ways to begin.

A.   The Biology of Aging

Every man desires to live long, but no man would be old.

Jonathan Swift

Some teachers and students will be particularly interested in aging from a biological perspective. And some of the questions they will find intriguing are these: How do different species of animals differ in life expectancy? How is it that each species, as well as each individual within a species, has a fixed life span? What makes some people live longer than others? What steps can we take to make sure that we remain healthy and that the last years of our lives are pleasurable and productive? What physiological changes are "normal" in the later years? How much variation is there from the norm? What are the physiological causes and concomitants of aging?

Students, of course, will deal with these questions very differently, depending on their age, their maturity, and their level of scientific sophistication. One thing they will all learn, however, is that as yet we have no one theory that can satisfactorily explain the aging process. Instead, we have several, each of which sheds some light on it.

Shock[1] provides us with a succinct and highly usable summary of aging theories. According to one genetic theory, he explains, cells die when damaged DNA molecules fail to provide them with the information they need in order to function and reproduce. Another genetic theory maintains that we age because when cells receive misinformation and fail to produce exact copy enzymes, they die. According to a third, people age because over time more and more cells undergo somatic mutations from radiation and other causes. Among the nongenetic theories, one holds that waste that cannot be eliminated gradually builds up in cells and eventually destroys them. A second sees age occurring when pairs of large molecules couple, or *cross-link*, with each other and when they clog the tissues and cells, interrupting their normal functioning. Another holds that the organs of the human body, like the parts of any machine, simply wear out from use and then cease to function. Some physiologists see stress build-up as the primary cause of aging. Others subscribe to the *single-organ theory*, pointing to the deterioration of one organ or one system, usually cardiovascular. Still others claim that the body's immune system begins to make errors, producing antibodies that kill healthy cells rather than protect them.

Of all these theories—genetic, nongenetic and physiological—the two that Shock sees as the most likely to produce a breakthrough—if not lead us to the Fountain of Youth—are the cross-link theory and the auto-immune theory. At the moment, however, all we can be reasonably certain of is that both life and death somehow depend on some kind of genetically programmed cellular clock.

Most students through their teens, we can assume, will have had few direct contacts with older people, and, therefore, we can expect them to have distorted ideas of the physical characteristics of the elderly. The child whose 81-year-old grandparent still goes to work every day, drives a car, and chops wood on weekends has a far different conception of what older people can do physically than does the child who sees his or her bedridden grandparent crippled by arthritis and emphysema.

Because neither films nor TV nor the comics will tell them, most students probably need to learn in school what senescence or "normal" aging really is. They may be surprised to learn that while older people are statistically more likely to die than young people, and while the elderly are more likely to suffer from a wide variety of fatal ailments, no one has ever actually "died of old age." They also need to learn that people grow old at very different rates, both as groups and as individuals. And they also need to learn that an individual may be quite old in some respects and quite young in others. They need to learn, in short, to be wary about generalizing on the basis of chronological age.

Recognizing the tremendous variability within and among older people should help alert students and better prepare them to cope with the kinds of biological change, usually deterioration, they will see in their grandparents, their parents, and later in themselves. They should learn that certain things happen physiologically to everyone who lives long enough. As we age, our skin dries out and becomes less elastic and more wrinkled and mottled; it also bruises easily and heals slowly. Our hair turns gray, then white, and falls out. Muscle tone declines. We lose subcutaneous fat and tissue and become more sensitive to changes in temperature. Our appetite wanes and we lose weight. As the cartilage between our spinal discs disappears, the spine compresses, and we become slightly shorter or, at least, we tend to bend over. Our bones become lighter and more porous and brittle. Our heart pumps less efficiently. Digestive juices flow less freely, peristalsis is weaker, and we have trouble digesting and eliminating. While the drive for sex, like the drives for food and activity, may abate somewhat, contrary to conventional belief, those well into and even beyond their seventies usually retain the capacity to have and enjoy sex.

Old people, students will learn, generally lose some of the sharpness in their senses, although here again there are enormous individual differences. Commonly people over 60 need more light and become "farsighted" (i.e., they see less well up close), and many develop cataracts which obscure the ocular lens. They also often lose some of their hearing, particularly their ability to hear high frequencies. It is also possible, though not so well established, that older people suffer losses in taste, smell, and touch. More certain, however, is that they have trouble keeping their equilibrium.

Reflexes, like the senses, also seem to decline with age. The older people get, the slower their reaction time, making them less able to cope with certain situations where immediate response is vital, like driving in traffic. Reflexes are never simply "automatic," and what may well handicap older persons is the larger backlog of experience to which they must refer before responding. Older people, research shows, are at an advantage in situations that call for accuracy, but they are at a disadvantage when situations call for quick, off-the-cuff judgments.

As teachers and students discuss sensory characteristics, perception, and reflexes, they move into an area where the boundary between the physiology and the psychology of aging blurs. Obviously much of an old person's mind-set—feelings, attitudes, personality, and self-image—flows from his or her bodily condition.

If students are to achieve an empathetic understanding of what it is to be old, they must feel what it is like to suffer from sensory deprivation or some other physical handicap. Older people who lose their capacity to taste or smell also often lose interest in eating. When they lose their sight or hearing, they become embarrassed and avoid stairs, traffic, and social situations. One method teachers can use to help students empathize with handicapped older persons is a method often used in training gerontological staff: students spend a day in a wheelchair, wear dark glasses that obscure their vision or blurred goggles that make the ground seem to heave, or wear earplugs and nose clips; i.e., they experience the world as so many older people eventually experience it.[2]

B. The Psychology of Aging

If wrinkles must be written upon our brows, let them not be written upon the heart. The spirit should not grow old.

James A. Garfield

Making predictions about the physiological development of older people is actually far less risky than making predictions about their psychological changes. If students learn only one thing from their study of aging, they should come away wary of glib generalizations. Aging males are not always "dirty old men," and many "old dogs" learn new tricks quite readily. If the extreme variability older people show biologically surprises students, they will be even more surprised at the variability the elderly show mentally and emotionally. Even as they learn some of the common syndromes and patterns of behavior one may expect among the aged, students will become alert to the complexities involved in explaining all human attitudes and behavior. They will come to appreciate both the extreme tentativeness with which one labels cause and effect and the idiosyncratic nature of each older person's situation.

One thing young people are often quite certain of—usually as a result of scant evidence—is how smart or how stupid old people generally are. Luckily, intelligence happens to be an area in which research has been plentiful and in which it also has solid things to say. Students should listen because they can learn much about both age and research. They can learn that testing during World War I with the Army Alpha Test and in the 1930's with the Wechsler Adult Intelligence Scale seemed to prove that intelligence peaked somewhere in a person's twenties and declined steadily thereafter.[1] These were cross-sectional studies, however, which may have proved only that different generations have different levels of intelligence, or at least that they score differently on particular intelligence tests. That this, indeed, was the case became evident in the 1950's when other researchers, using longitudinal methods (i.e., testing the same individuals over the course of their lifetimes), proved that as long as people remain reasonably healthy, as they age they show no decrease in general mental ability.[2]

With memory the picture is not quite so clear. Most studies show that older people do less well than younger people with items that call for short-term memory, but that they do about equally well with items that call for long-term memory. How much of this deficit can be attributed to testing situations that fail to motivate older people or that demand speedy responses is hard to tell. How much of it is the result of purposeful forgetting, a screening out of what they wish to forget, is hard to tell. And how much of it is the result of a self-fulfilling prophecy—we are expected to lose our memory as we age— is also hard to know. Two centuries ago Samuel Johnson said it well:

> There is a wicked inclination in most people to suppose an old man decayed in his intellect. If a young or middle-aged man, when leaving a company, does not recollect where he laid his hat, it is nothing; but if the same inattention is discovered in an old man, people will shrug their shoulders and say, "His memory is going."[3]

Particularly now in a period of economic stress, older people are being asked, or are being forced, to leave their jobs and make room for younger workers. Secondary school students, who will soon be trying to enter the work place themselves, should know something about how capable older workers actually are and what forced retirement means to them. They should know that, by and large, older workers do not match the stereotype—that their performance, on average, is as good as or better than that of younger workers.[4] Longitudinal evidence is meager, but if older workers, as they age, become slower and less strong than their younger counterparts, they also compensate or more than compensate by becoming more experienced, more accurate, and more committed. Their absentee rates are lower; they get sick or injured less often. And since they are more satisfied with their current jobs, they are less restless and less likely to leave.[5] One empirical study demonstrates that historians and philosophers are most productive in their sixties and that scholars in general, excluding scientists, produce at 90 percent of peak efficiency when they are in their seventies.[6] Pablo Casals, Picasso, and Grandma Moses, all of whom worked prodigiously in their nineties, support the point rather emphatically.

Another aspect of life among the elderly which most young people are blissfully unaware of is the fact that the later years, like the earlier ones, are stressful, and often extremely so. From a young person's perspective, other than death, a grandparent has no crises to face and has probably by now come to terms even with death. Certainly a grandparent can now relax with no critical decisions to make, no more mountains to climb or dragons to slay. How far from the truth. Alarming evidence of how stressful the later years actually are is the fact that older people, who account for only 10 percent of our population, commit 25 percent of reported suicides.[7] (If we were also to include the suicides of those who kill themselves by refusing food or medicine, the proportion would be even higher.) Another telling statistic reveals that among white males, the suicide rate rises steadily with each age decade, even through the eighties.[8]

Much of the stress in old age comes, of course, from a succession of losses old people suffer, the magnitude of which often goes unnoticed, particularly by younger people. Students who see the calm exterior of older people may fail to realize how hard it is for them to cope with the loss of a mate, of close family, of friends, of a job, of financial independence, of mobility, of physical capacities, of "good looks," of familiar living arrangements, of any one or all of these. Then add the greatest loss of all, the imminent loss of life itself. Before students can learn to understand what it is to grow old, they need to understand, first, that these are the losses and stresses of later life and, second, that there are ways of coping and of not coping with them.

Students generally know one or more old people who are mentally or emotionally unbalanced. The "crazy old coot" down the street with a house full of cats who keeps the blinds drawn looms large in their minds. They are unlikely to know that only 15 percent of our elderly show any significant psychopathology and that age brings no real increase in mental disorders.[9] They are also not likely to know the distinction between organic and functional disorders, and are prone to pass off any aberrant behavior on the part of older people as "senility." Hopefully one thing we can do is discourage our classes from using the term *senile* as indiscriminately as the general public does and as even many health professionals now do.[10] Our students can learn that senility is *not* inevitable, is not a normal part of aging, and is certainly not a term to apply to an older person who is merely forgetful, confused, or withdrawn.

Students should realize that in view of their actual and impending losses, older people can be expected occasionally to show signs of depression. Therefore, students should learn what some of the common signs of depression are. They should learn to recognize when older people appear unusually sad, disinterested, pessimistic, and inconclusive, and they should be alert to the slowed speech and body movements and to the lack of appetite and insomnia of many older people.

To the extent that they can, students should also gain some awareness of the typical methods old people employ to handle their losses and their frustrations. Usually, Butler and Lewis say, old people use the same methods they found useful when they were younger: most commonly, in technical jargon, counterphobia, displacement, projection, selective memory, and the "Peter Pan" technique.[11] Those who are counterphobic willfully disregard both obvious symptoms and medical advice (e.g., they shovel wet snow after a heart attack). Some find they cope better by displacing, or transferring, the reason for their troubles to a person, object, or event outside themselves (e.g., their physician, the stock market, or the weather). Others may accuse storekeepers or even close family members of cheating and trying to hurt them. By projecting onto others the feelings and ideas that they must reject in themselves, they experience some relief. Others through a highly selective memory pick and choose to remember out of the past only what was pleasant or what supports their positive self-image. Still others adapt by denial: like Peter Pan, they never grow old or at least insist to themselves, as well as others, that age has bypassed them personally.

Psychologists have categorized the personalities of older people into types, some of whom they feel age "well" and others "poorly." One such categorization lists three types of men who age well: (1) the "mature men," those who look back on their lives as having been well spent and look ahead to continued social participation; (2) the "rocking chair men," those who are glad to be rid of responsibilities and relish "taking it easy"; and (3) the "armored men," those who put aging out of their mind and plug on as actively as they can. The two types that adapt poorly to aging are (1) the "angry men," those who feel their lives were a failure and blame others for it; and (2) the "self-haters," those who also feel their lives were unsuccessful but who blame themselves for it.[12]

Helping students to understand the variety of ways in which old people adapt to their age is not, of course, an attempt to provide them with a gerontological how-to-do-it manual. But such understanding bears on the general human condition, and, more pragmatically it can provide at least a first step for students who are trying to deal humanely and intelligently with the old people who do come into their own lives. When grandpa, for the umpteenth time, begins to tell the story of how he "met up with a wildcat," the student may be more understanding, recognizing that for all of us one essential part of coming to terms with old age, as well as with death, is reviewing one's life and finding meaning in it. As Butler and Lewis say:

Some of the positive results of reviewing one's life can be a righting of old wrongs, making up with enemies, coming to acceptance of mortal life, a sense of serenity, pride in accomplishment, and feeling of having done one's best. It gives people an opportunity to decide what to do with the time left to them and work out emotional and material legacies. People become ready but in no hurry to die. Possibly the qualities of serenity, philosophical development, and wisdom observable in some older people reflect a state of resolution of their life conflicts.[13]

Any teacher who can help students understand more fully what it means to grow old helps not only those who are now old but also those who will be, including the students themselves.

C. Aging: The View from History

> The experience of aging has also changed faster than our under-
> standing of it. Growing old in America today (and increasingly
> throughout the world) is an experience profoundly different from
> what it was two or three centuries ago.
>
> *David Hackett Fischer*

To prepare for the future by studying the past, says Marshall
McLuhan, is like driving a car with your eyes on the rear-view mirror. The analogy is clever but more wrong than right. History, it is
true, seldom repeats itself, but the future invariably depends on the
past. Knowing history may not enable us to predict the future, but it
certainly better prepares us for what the future will bring. If we learn
from the past what efforts have already been made and with what
results, as a society we are more likely to set goals that are feasible and
that reflect our values and, also, to adopt realistic means for their
achievement.

History, or more accurately the teaching of history, has changed
drastically during recent decades. What was once almost exclusively a
concern with diplomatic, military, and political events has given way
to a strong emphasis on social, intellectual, and cultural affairs. Students learn about cabbages as well as kings, and it would be quite in
keeping with the aims of today's enlightened social studies curriculums that they learn how people grew old in earlier times and how
earlier generations related to one another. Such knowledge can help
us as we face up to the fact that we, too, both as individuals and as a
society, have our own serious problems of aging.

Surprisingly much is known about old age in the prehistoric and
ancient worlds, and we and our students have access to a wealth of
rich materials. Historian David Fischer sums up what at first appears
to be a mass of conflicting information in four pithy generalizations:

> First, people of advanced age were very rare. The extreme limit
> of life was much the same as in the modern world but few people
> lived to reach it . . . . Second, although few reached the age of
> fifty in those societies, there were always people who were per-
> ceived to be old . . . . Third, these "old" people were treated
> in ways which were invested with the authority of sacred obliga-
> tion . . . . Fourth, there was another stage of life beyond that
> of "elder" . . . . Even as most primitive societies honored their
> elders, many societies (though not all) showed little mercy

toward senility or decrepitude. When the old were no longer able to contribute to the common welfare and no longer able to look after themselves, they were often destroyed.[1]

When the great civilizations of the Mediterranean crescent, the Middle and the Far East came on the scene, Fischer adds, they discontinued the practice of *senecide* (i.e., the destruction of nonproductive or senile elders). Able to pass knowledge on from generation to generation via the written word, these later societies did not depend on the elders to perform this function and were affluent enough to support them even when they became noncontributors. Generally speaking, however, most elders—who were actually young by our standards—needed no help. They often ran these civilizations. Age was respected, even revered, and it entitled one, at least if he was a male and a member of the elite, to power and property. Government and the family were both gerontocracies in which the young deferred to the old and suffered if they did not.

During the Middle Ages, age relations changed little, and as the Catholic Church grew, it, too, assumed all the characteristics of a gerontocracy. In England as well as on the continent and as far as the Orient, age demanded and continued to get its due.

After the Middle Ages, historical resources on aging available to us thin out appreciably. Since then some sociologists, economists, political scientists, and psychologists have been active, but as of 1977, Fischer says flatly that the historical cupboard is bare: "No modern history of old age has been published in any western language. The subject has suffered almost total neglect at the hands of historians."[2] He then proceeds to help fill the gap by writing a brilliant, if contentious, history of aging in America. His scholarly little volume *Growing Old in America* reads like a novel and is invaluable not only for those who would teach about aging but also for any teacher or student of American history.

Fischer frankly distrusts the conventional explanation of how the elderly came to their currently low status in America. This explanation holds that as the world became a healthier place, old people multiplied in proportion to the general population, making most of them redundant in the work force. Cities grew, the extended family unit broke down, and old people lost their major source of economic as well as psychosocial support. As the masses became literate and educated and as technology rapidly expanded, older people no longer had the special knowledge and expertise that had brought them respect and often veneration. Fischer, however, finds this explanation plausible but leaky. Recent studies convince him that the nuclear family actually predates our urban, industrial society. Also, the fact that the elderly in Japan have retained most of their traditional eminence suggests that modernization—basically urban living and industrialization—need not be at the expense of the elderly.

The experience of aging in America, it is obvious, has changed drastically since colonial days. Then to be old was to be exalted. With age came authority in the church, in the family, in politics, and in the marketplace. It was a gerontocracy that kept the young in a state of dependence on the old, a condition that fostered respect, however, rather than warmth. While stable because they were clear, relationships between the generations often lacked affect, and people who grew old could count more on sustained dignity and on financial security than they could on love and sympathy.

Somewhere about 1800, age relations took a turn which has continued to this day. The cult of age gradually transformed itself into a cult of youth, and then old age, as Fischer puts it, for the first time in our history became a problem. As more and more people lived to a ripe old age, to be old was no longer a distinction. Parents outlived their children's dependency, people stopped powdering their hair and trying to look older, and preferred seats in church went not to the old but to those who could pay the price.[3]

As primogeniture disappeared and one could acquire wealth through means other than owning land, sons gained their independence earlier. Older workers found themselves forced to retire before they felt either ready or able to, and writers like Henry Thoreau began to deplore old age and demean older people. In short, a kind of gerontophobia took over, paving the way for today's Pepsi generation.

Setting it deftly in the context of American history, Fischer then describes the experience of older people in modern times. He traces the rapid growth in forced retirement and consequent poverty among the aged, the growing isolation of the elderly, the establishment of "poor farms" and other age-segregated retirement communities, the battle for old-age pensions, the "Ham and Eggs" movement, and the Townsend Plan. He describes the introduction of social security and the organizing of pressure groups (the National Retired Teachers Association, the American Association of Retired Persons, and the National Caucus of the Black Aged), the Older Americans Act (1965), medicare and medicaid (1965), and the three White House Conferences on Aging (1961, 1971, and 1981). He concludes with some highly practical suggestions to reform our program of social welfare and to keep our social security system from either collapsing or becoming an intolerable burden on the young.

I have dwelt on Fischer's work at some length, first, because it is the only full-length perspective on U.S. age relations by a modern historian and, second, because the book establishes so clearly the fact that to understand America, one must understand the story of its elderly. Conversely, one cannot begin to solve aging problems in America without studying the total spectrum of American social history. When Fischer describes the worldwide social revolution that took place at the end of the eighteenth and the beginning of the nineteenth centuries and that included the American and French revolutions, he points sharply at the usually overlooked but key role age relations play in the course of human history:

> Every sort of human relations was transformed by it: relations between nations, classes, races, sexes—and also generations. The great revolution was, among other things, a revolution in age relations. It was the end of an *ancien regime* which was also a *regime des anciens* . . . . On the surface it introduced a spirit of age equality . . . . But beneath that surface a new sort of inequality was born, a new hierarchy of generations in which youth acquired the moral advantage that age had lost.[4]

D.   The Politics and Economics of Aging

> Over one-third of the black elderly still live in poverty. . . . We see a people who continue to suffer the ravages of poor health, inadequate diet and poor housing. We witness the continuing mortality rates among black men that leave black women alone, vulnerable and poor.
>
> *Dr. Aaron Henry*

At various times during their precollege schooling, students analyze the American political system and the workings of its economy. At some point in this study their attention could well be directed to the role now played, and potentially to be played, by the senior citizen segment that is now 10 percent of our voting population and rapidly expanding. Laswell calls politics the art or science of deciding who gets what, when, and how.[1] Therefore, classes that deal with aging, particularly those in social studies, should lead students to inquire into the extent to which older people actually participate in the political process, the nature of their political views, their impact on the system, and also what they themselves get out of it. In looking at our economy, students should explore whether older people share equitably in society's allocation of what are always scarce goods and services, and how, as senior citizens, they make out in the world of work and then after they leave it.

Because so many young people hold a "rocking chair" stereotype of the elderly, they are generally surprised by the high level of political activity citizens over 65 display. The fact that youth—actually a small minority of youth—has been active and highly vocal in recent years on controversial issues (Viet Nam, the draft, abortion, legalization of marijuana) tends to obscure the equally salient fact that young people actually exercise their voting privilege less than do their parents and far less than do their grandparents. For example, in the 1976 presidential election only 36 percent of males and 40 percent of females in the 18–20 age bracket voted; in the 65–74 age bracket, in spite of ill health and lack of mobility, 71 percent of eligible men and 63 percent of eligible women made their way to the polls.[2] This remarkable voting activity, researchers suggest, reflects a rising level of political interest on the part of older people as their involvement in career and family lessens.[3]

Students are also often surprised at the ages of people who are still active in public office. It was Francis Bacon who once said: "Young men are fitter to invent than to judge, fitter for execution than for counsel; and fitter for new projects than for settled business."[4] Apparently Americans, in spite of their adoration of youth, would agree. For our top positions of leadership, as Presidents, Supreme Court Justices, Senators, Representatives, and governors, we choose a disproportionate number of senior citizens. Also, the higher the office, the older the person we are likely to choose for it. With no mandatory retirement age, federal judges usually serve until a ripe old age, and often until they die in office. When it suited our mood, we elected 43-year-old John Kennedy to be President, but 20 years later advanced age proved no handicap, and was perhaps even an asset, to Ronald Reagan, whom we elected by a landslide.

The possibility of an "old people's liberation" or a "senior power" movement which would exercise a decisive political influence is an idea that appeals to aging activists and that may also intrigue students. Although they constitute only 10 percent of the voting population, people over 65 now do 16 percent of the voting, and every year they become a larger proportion of the body politic.[5] In Florida and Arizona, and in particular electoral districts in other states where they live in large numbers, they already exercise strong political clout, and analysts point to particular elections in which their voting has proved decisive. On the other hand, there are reasons for questioning whether the aged will ever vote as a single-minded power bloc. First of all, it is likely that for many years to come Americans generally will continue to view age negatively. As a result, older people will continue to deny their aging, and many will refuse to identify with "the elderly." Second, as people become senior citizens, they always retain strong prior identifications based on such factors as race, religion, ethnic background, social class, occupation, and residence—varied and at times conflicting identifications that are more likely than age to determine how an older person votes on candidates and issues.

Conventional wisdom has it that as they age, people become more conservative. Younger people commonly assume that part of becoming old is to become more conservative, less open to change. It is true that more so than do the young, older people oppose busing for school integration, legalizing marijuana, expanding women's rights, and raising school taxes.[6] But taking these positions does not necessarily mean that older people have grown more conservative as they have aged. What young people—and many older ones as well—need to learn is the significance of what sociologists call the *cohort effect*. Briefly, people behave as they do in large measure due to the age cohort in which they were born and were then socialized.

> Data on persons who are old at the time of measurement may reveal more about the shared experiences and perceptions of that particular older generation . . . than about anything intrinsic to the process of aging.[7]

Older people often take what is currently labelled a "conservative" position not because they have become any less liberal as they have aged but simply because the world itself has moved on since their youth to a more permissive stance.

Then, too, it is good for students to learn that *liberal* and *conservative* are slippery terms which require definition if they are to further rather than obscure communication. For example, were senior citizens being liberal when, more often than people under 65, they took a "dovish" stand on Viet Nam? Or were they merely being consistent in their isolationism? Are they liberal now when they demand increases in federally supported medical programs, and are they conservative when they vote against school aid? Or in both cases are they simply voting out of economic self-interest? It is true that in the 1980 presidential election, liberal third-party candidate John Anderson attracted proportionately more young than old voters. It is also true, however, that in 1968 it was young rather than old voters who supported George Wallace and his segregationist platform.

Historically the "haves," those who have the most to conserve, have been more conservative politically than the "have-nots." This has led to the myth that older people are more conservative than the young, and that they become more so *as* they age and *because* of their aging. When highly visible rebels of the 60's age and settle in the suburbs, and when Abby Hoffman puts on a vest and takes a job on Wall Street, they seem to dramatize the point. But the point is not that simple. One well-documented study actually indicates that "people have typically become less, rather than more conservative as they grow older."[8] Hopefully students in aging classes will come to understand the complexity of this age–attitude relationship; if they do so, they are more likely to distrust other pat statements about age as well as other stereotypes.

When a curriculum calls for study of the role that pressure groups play in our political system, it should include an analysis of lobbies for the elderly along with those for labor, industry, and the professions. Students should know what power the AFL-CIO, the NAM, the NEA, the AMA, and the VFW wield and what political stands they take. And they should also learn something about the three mass membership organizations that represent senior citizens: the National Association of Retired Federal Employees (NARFE), the National Council of Senior Citizens (NCSC), and the National Retired Teachers Association and American Association of Retired Persons (NRTA-AARP). They should know, for example, that while the NRTA-AARP is nonpartisan, the NCSC allies itself with the Democratic party; that the basically middle class NRTA-AARP opposes any ceiling on earnings by social security recipients, while the NCSC, basically working class, lobbies to retain a ceiling; that although both organizations argue for a national health care plan, labor-minded NCSC favors a national health security plan, which the NRTA-AARP views as socialized medicine; that the NRTA-AARP, which has long had connections with the insurance industry, would much prefer a greatly expanded medicare program.[9]

Students should also have some knowledge of the Gray Panthers, a relatively small but potent organization. Led by charismatic Maggie Kuhn and open to younger as well as older members, the Panthers call

Golden Age Clubs "playpens for the old" and publicly announce that they are out to radicalize the elderly. "We are not mellow, sweet old people," says Kuhn. "We have got to effect change and we have nothing to lose."[10] For a secondary school social studies class, the Panthers present a fascinating case study of a grass-roots, offbeat, militantly political movement. Students can debate whether on balance it is an advantage or a disadvantage for the Panthers to have a leader as charismatic as Maggie Kuhn, and whether in the long run they are helping or hurting the cause of the elderly when they welcome the nonelderly to join them and when they join their allies to fight against not only mandatory retirement but also militarism, racism, sexism, and even J.P. Stevens' labor policy. Jacobs and Hess laud the Panthers as

> . . . raising consciousness, questioning the most sacred of American values, and ultimately giving us an example of effective aging: to care enough to fight, to risk being thought silly, to work for those goals which will enhance the quality of life throughout the life course.[11]

Students can question whether the Panthers must inevitably compromise their principles, as they did when they accepted a $16,000 U.S. Administration on Aging grant; whether their broad-gauged attack on "the system" is quixotic rather than realistic; and whether they will last as an organization and eventually have a significant impact on the quality of life elderly Americans lead, or disappear, without effect, as have so many other meteoric do-good movements.

Students who are primarily interested in the economics of aging have a multitude of topics they can research and discuss: Why has the proportion of older males in our work force declined steadily since 1900 whereas the proportion of women over 65 has remained stable?[12] Do workers become more or less productive in their later years? Why do older workers have difficulty finding jobs? Is a retirement policy, either mandatory or flexible, in the best interests of the worker? Of society? For whom is early retirement a good thing? What kind of preparations should one make for retirement? Is retirement harder on men than on women?

In America why are 14 percent of our elderly living below the poverty level? What sources of income do people over 65 depend on? How did our social security system originate, and how does it compare with those in other countries? Is it a dole or is it insurance? Who are entitled to what social security benefits? Who pays what social security taxes? Why is the system in jeopardy, and what remedies have been suggested for its rescue and improvement? Now that government rather than family tends to provide the aged with economic support and now that middle-aged workers, still supporting their own children, are being taxed to provide current retiree benefits, how have personal relationships between the elderly and their children been affected?[13] Is an important connection between generations lost when older people depend more on government than on children and grandchildren for funds? Does this reduce contact and increase alienation, or, on the other hand, does this reduce conflict and improve relations? These are highly debatable questions, and they represent only a small sample of those that precollege classes in aging can profitably explore.

E. Aging: A Sociological Perspective

In highly industrialized societies, older persons are seen as economic burdens since they are relegated to the nonworking and become more dependent on services rather than being producers themselves
John C. Morgan

When sociologists focus their tools on the elderly as one stratum of the population, they are working in the field of either *social gerontology* or *sociology of aging.* Those who call themselves *social gerontologists* may be trained in any one of several disciplines and are likely to have applied interests, whereas those who see themselves as *sociologists of aging* almost invariably are professionally trained sociologists with more theoretical interests. The distinction between the two "disciplines" remains fuzzy, but both attempt, via the scientific method, to understand the interaction of older people among themselves and with others.

Sociologists and social gerontologists alike use three basic research techniques: the sample survey, the case study, and the experiment. Even in elementary school classes it is not too early for students to familiarize themselves with all three of these research methods, to design and take part in such research, and to begin to understand how to interpret the results. One of the best ways to study social science at any level, it is generally agreed, is to *do* it. And imaginative precollege teachers can and have designed learning experiences in which students of all ages play the role of social scientist. Before they begin their own research, however, students might profit from studying a model survey such as that done by Louis Harris in 1974 on public expectations of aging.[1] Or they might read case studies like Hochschild's on old people in retirement communities.[2] Or they might look at experiments such as that which Auerbach and Levenson designed to test the effects of social contact on the anti-age bias of students.[3]

At first blush, demography may appear to be an arid and forbidding subject for precollege students. It needn't be. Many of the problems demographers deal with actually fascinate youngsters and adolescents. What makes particular populations grow or decline, move or age, can intrigue social studies or math classes. People of all ages are also curious about those who live extraordinarily long lives; they relish stories about mountain villages in Ecuador, the Caucasus, and Kashmir where both men and women routinely live beyond the age of one hundred. Students want to know whether Americans live longer than Swedes or Russians or Chinese, and whether whites live longer than blacks or Chicanos, and, if so, why. They will also be interested in where most old people in America live—in what sections of the country, in what kinds of housing, and with whom. They will be interested in the puzzling problem—and it is a problem—of why women everywhere outlive men. They will enjoy entertaining the hypothesis that as the life-style of women comes closer and closer to that of men, this discrepancy in longevity between the sexes will begin to disappear. These areas that interest professional demographers can also provide provocative data for analysis in precollege social studies and math classes.

Another area of interest for the sociologist is that of age norms. Children and adolescents are constantly reminded, both by adults and by their peer group, of what constitutes age-appropriate behavior. The elderly, too, are expected to behave in societally determined ways. This comes as a surprise to many young people. Realizing that older people, too, must choose between becoming what is expected of them and rebelling against society's ideas of what is "normal" for them may help some young people understand and cope with their own age-norm pressures. Seeing one's problems as others experience them can often be salutary. Stepping into new roles as one moves from one age status to another can be traumatic, we know, for young people. But the rites of passage American society provides for transitting into old age are even fewer and less well defined than those it provides at earlier stages in the life cycle.[4] Thus, becoming "old" can also be traumatic. Once they are able to empathize with the old, the

47

young will learn much about themselves as well as the old from looking carefully at the variety of ways in which older people relate to the
fact of becoming old.

A society like ours, one that places a high premium on values such
as independence, work, action, youth, education, and progress, makes
life particularly difficult for its elderly. If young people are to learn
not only what American values are but also how they impact on various subgroups in our society, they will come to understand how our
subscription, and at times our addiction, to the Protestant work ethic
has adversely affected the lives and self-image of Americans in retirement. They will come to realize how our valuing of independence,
action, youth, education, and progress, although it accounts for much
of our nation's greatness, also accounts for our devaluing of age and
the elderly. As a group, our elderly are not only less youthful than the
general population but also less independent, less active, and less educated, and for these reasons, regrettably, we value them less. Our
students might well begin thinking now of how best to prepare themselves for an old age in which they can be maximally independent,
active, youthful, and educated, and therefore maximally valued.
They might also try wrestling with the problem of how to develop
more positive attitudes on the part of others toward the elderly and
the values they represent. In so doing, consciously or not, students will
be working in their own eventual self-interest.

Many precollege students have grandparents or close relatives who
are retired or widowed. Despite the experience young people themselves have in moving from childhood into adolescence, it is not easy
for them to understand what these older people go through when they
retire and are forced to vacate roles they have occupied for years.
What young people fail to realize is that, at every previous stage,
when one discards a role, one always assumes another (e.g., one moves
from student to employee or from single person to married person),
but a person who retires or is widowed in our society assumes an ambiguous or undefined role—what Burgess called "a roleless role":

> The retired older man and his wife are imprisoned in a roleless
> role. They have no vital functions to perform. . . . Nor are they
> offered a ceremonial role by society to make up in part for their
> lost functional role.[5]

Those who subscribe to the *disengagement theory* of aging suggest
that older people and society, to their mutual advantage, should grad-

ually withdraw from each other.[6] On the other hand, proponents of the *activity theory* hold that this withdrawal is really one-sided, that older people should withdraw only under pressure, and that their best interests are really served by continuing to be active in their usual role, or at least in a substitute one, as long as possible.[7] Society today reflects this disengagement–activity conflict and gives older people mixed signals. But young people also get mixed signals: they find that they are old enough to work, to marry, to have children, and even to die in battle, but they are not old enough to by beer. Again, any class that clarifies the problems older people have with role ambiguity can help students better relate to older people they know themselves, and it can also help them accept and perhaps better cope with their own youthful role ambiguities.

Living with a family is not always easy for young people. Learning something about the history of the American family, its functioning, and the roles people old and young have played in it may or may not make their lives any easier, but children and adolescents at least will need no coaxing to study a subject they already have a vital interest in. They may be surprised to learn, among other things, that despite what their parents or grandparents or even their history books say, what made "the good old days" good was not the large, extended family, all living cozily together at the old homestead. Research now strongly suggests that "the nuclear parent–child family has always been the model family type in the United States and that three generation families have always been relatively rare."[8] As Goode says, "We now *see* more large old houses than small ones; they survived longer because they were likely to have been better constructed. The one-room cabins rotted away."[9] Students can also learn that the "alienation" of older people today from their families, if not a myth, is at least a distortion. Figures show that only one out of five of today's elderly is childless, and researchers have found that the overwhelming majority of older people maintain regular contact with their children by visit or by phone.[10]

Students will be interested in the kinds of financial and other mutual aid old and young family members provide each other in different social classes and in different ethnic groups. They will also be interested in the variety of relationships grandparents can have with grandchildren—e.g., Neugarten and Weinstein identify five types of grandparent: the *formal*, the *fun-seeking*, the *surrogate parent*, the *fount-of-wisdom*, and the *distant* types.[11] Some students, particularly elementary-age children, may want to take part in the nationwide, federally funded Foster Grandparents program. In doing so, not only they but also their "foster grandparents" stand to gain. Teachers of more mature students may choose to discuss various alternatives to the traditional family which have been tried by the elderly and which some sociologists now suggest. I refer, for example, to the commune, in which several older people of both sexes choose to live together; to polygamy, in which an older man has several wives, thereby reducing the surplus of widows; and to cohabitation, which may solve certain economic problems but raise serious psychological ones.[12]

One of youth's many problems is how to gain acceptance in a social group, how to be nourished and yet not dominated by the group. Adolescence, in a sense, constitutes a culture or subculture of its own: adolescents cluster together at school and have their own music, language, dress, hangouts, and recreational activities. Although many other sociologists disagree, Arnold Rose maintains that older Americans similarly constitute a subculture, one that cuts across religious, racial, ethnic, and sex lines. Whether they fit the classic definition of a subculture or not, the elderly are often segregated from other age groups, they tend to interact largely or exclusively with each other, and they have something of a common history, strong common interests, and an increasingly strong sense of group identification. The result is that individual elders, like adolescents and pre-adolescents, feel pressure to conform to group norms, and they, too, must decide when to join and when not to join, when to acquiesce and when to resist.

A course or unit on aging taught from a sociological perspective should also spend some time on the voluntary associations established for and by older people as well as on those that provide services for the elderly. By the time they leave high school, young people should know what the NRTA-AARP, the NCSC, and the Gray Panthers are. They should know what roles older people play in ACTION programs like the Retired Senior Volunteer Program (RSVP), Service Corps of Retired Executives (SCORE), Volunteers in Service to America (VISTA), the Peace Corps, and Foster Grandparents. And they should know what services medicare, medicaid, the Visiting Nurses Association (VNA), Meals on Wheels, and the senior citizens centers provide. Well-informed citizens of all ages need to know about these agencies, and as the only institution that reaches all people, the school should see to it that all students have at least a basic familiarity with them.

F.   Literature and Aging

No Spring nor Summer Beauty hath such grace
As I have seen in one Autumnal face.

John Donne

Both from casual observation and from well-documented research we know that young people today have essentially negative attitudes toward the elderly and toward their own aging. We also know that young people today have few face-to-face contacts with older people and that the few they do have are often limited to visits with grandparents or other aging relatives. How then do they acquire these negative attitudes? This is not an easy question. Some of the answer may be genetic or instinctive: it may be natural to recoil from the image of our own inevitable aging, dying, and death. Some of it, however, must be experiential, must be behavior learned from the environment. It stands to reason that how students react to the way older people look and behave and how they anticipate their own aging depend significantly on cues they get from their family, peers, teachers, and also the media.

The assumption is commonly made that the media are influential in determining many of the attitudes and stereotypes we develop, including those on aging. This assumption is so difficult to test—because so many intervening variables exist—that researchers usually confine themselves to content analysis; that is, they analyze and/or quantify the content of films, magazines, newspapers, advertising, song lyrics, and literature, and then they simply assume that the content, acting as a stimulus, reflects itself in audience attitudes, whether creating, reinforcing, altering, or even reversing them.

Teachers of literature at all levels also work on the assumption that the books students read actually *do* make a difference, that the books they as teachers choose for students and the way they teach them make a difference in how students see themselves and see their world. It follows, then, that teachers of reading and literature who are also seriously concerned with how young people approach aging and the elderly should be keenly aware of how the books they teach—as well as those they choose *not* to teach—actually treat aging. In recent years teachers have shown laudable concern over the treatment blacks, ethnic minorities, and women receive. Now that ageism has been recognized as a societal ill, it is high time that teachers and parents paid equal concern to ageist biases in the books students read.

51

In 1977 Barnum analyzed 100 children's books at random and found clear-cut evidence of age discrimination.[1] First, she found that older people are conspicuous by their absence; they made an appearance far less often than their numbers in the U.S. population would call for. And second, far more than their actual condition warrants, they are described as physically debilitated and socioeconomically deprived. Barnum then looked critically at the scant body of K–3 children's literature that does feature old people as major characters and found that it generally shows older males and females in stereotypical roles—older women cooking and keeping house, older men working outdoors or taking children on fishing trips. Rarely do children in literature spend time with old people to whom they are unrelated, and old people do most of the little socializing they do inside the home, seldom going out to theaters, clubs, or political meetings. Barnum found most elderly characters two-dimensional and too many of them passive or incompetent. As a consequence, she says:

> The young child learns from these books unfortunate lessons about old people: that they are not active or interesting, that old age is a period of restricted social activity, and that unless they are relatives, one does not associate with them. The result then is that these negative characteristics help produce or reinforce society's negative stereotypes about old age.[2]

Grim as old age may be, children's books almost without exception picture the relationship between grandparents and grandchildren as a warm one. Constant's study[3] shows that from old favorite *Heidi* (1884) to current favorites like Buckley's *Grandfather and I* (1959), Borack's *Grandpa* (1967), and Shulevitz's *Dawn* (1974), they almost invariably portray oldsters and youngsters empathetically sharing good times together. This seems to be the case whether the grandparent is senile (Blue's *Grandma Didn't Wave Back* and Lundgren's *Matt's Grandfather*); dying (Miska Miles' *Annie and the Old One*, de Paola's *Nana Upstairs, Nana Downstairs*, and Zolotow's *My Grandson Lew*); stereotyped (de Paola's *Watch Out for the Chicken Feet in Your Soup*); nonsexist (Zolotow's *William's Doll* and Williams' *Kevin's Grandma*); a swinger (Klein's *Taking Sides*); a friend (Klein's *Naomi in the Middle*); or a stranger (Skorpen's *Mandy's Grandmother* and Blume's *Are You There God? It's Me, Margaret*). The only prominent exception is Blume's *Blubber*, in which a granddaughter lashes out at her grandmother. Constant concludes that grandparents in today's children's books stereotypically respond warmly to their grandchildren, which leads her to wonder, understandably, how long this age of naturalism will last before children's authors begin to portray the relationship in a less idyllic and more realistic vein.

Other researchers see in children's literature rich resources for teaching about aging. Seefeldt and others find that through careful book selection "children can have the opportunity to see elderly persons in diverse roles, activities and life styles."[4] They point to books that go well beyond the warm child–grandparent bond. In Goffstein's *Fish For Supper* grandma gets up at five to go fishing; in Zolotow's *William's Doll* grandma is the only one to accept the fact that a boy may need a doll; in Williams' *Kevin's Grandma* grandma rides a Honda and goes sky diving and still has time to love and care for Kevin. Not all children's books sidestep conflict between old and young: witness Skorpen's *Mandy's Grandmother* and *The Secret Life of T.K. Dearing*. Some, like Lexau's *Benjie on His Own*, Schoettle's *Grandpa's Long Underwear*, and Sonneborn's *I Love Gram*, can help children cope with grandparents who are ill; and others, like Lundgren's *Matt's Grandfather*, Rabin's *Changes*, and Mazer's *A Figure of Speech*, with those who are senile. Others discuss the death of grandparents: e.g., Zolotow's *My Grandson Lew*; de Paola's *Nana Upstairs, Nana Downstairs*, and Miles' *Annie and the Old One*.

Children also need to know about old people besides grandparents if they are to know what varied lives the elderly actually live. To display older people nongrandparenting, Seefeldt and her colleagues recommend Estes' *The Middle Moffat*, Copeland's *Meet Miki Takino*, Keating's *Mr. Chu*, Smith's *Josie's Handful of Quietness*, Mathis' *The Hundred Penny Box*, and de Jong's *Journey from Peppermint Street*. To illustrate the fact that many older people are still making valuable contributions to society, they recommend de Paola's *Strega Nona*, Hodge's *The Wave*, Houston's *The White Archer: An Eskimo Legend*, and Haley's *A Story, A Story: An African Tale*. To help with the stresses of growing older themselves, children might read Krauss' *Growing Strong*, McCloskey's *One Morning in Maine*, Warburg's *Growing Time*, and Martin's *Knots on a Counting Rope*.

With adolescent literature the same problems and the same possibilities exist. David Peterson, Director of the Gerontology Program at the University of Nebraska (Omaha), and Elizabeth Karnes, Curriculum Coordinator at Father Flanagan's Boys' Home, have done the most comprehensive study to date of aging as portrayed in adolescent literature. Using for data 53 Newberry Award-winning books since 1922, they give the literature mixed reviews. On the one hand, they find no pattern of overt discrimination against older characters: most of them are not senile, decrepit, or sick; they are not excluded from stories; and they are not exclusively grandparents. They are rich and poor, wise and stupid, and lazy and energetic, and are portrayed positively or negatively depending on the individual. In other words, explicitly negative images are not prevalent. Peterson and Karnes, however, go on to say

> What may be more important than the direct negative stereotyping is the indirect picture of the older population. . . . Older people were portrayed as only shadows who moved in and out of the major flow of the story at expeditious times. They were not within the mainstream of the plot; they were the bit players who inhabited the fringes of the stage and who received neither the love nor the hate of the heroes or the villains.[5]

Authors of adolescent literature, it should be remembered, do not presume to be advocates for the elderly and only try to present the world as they perceive it. It is not, then, surprising that older characters resemble older people in America today and that Peterson and Karnes find that

> . . . older people seldom really existed in the eyes of others but quietly wandered through the pages, without trouble, gratification or suffering. . . . They are only partial people; they are not developed; they are not necessary to the real action that transpires about them. They are useful only for their relationship with the important people. In short, they are there, but no one seems to notice.[6]

That adolescent literature seldom features older characters should not be surprising. Adolescents are more interested in adolescents, and writers write for the market.

No teacher thinking about working with adolescent literature as it depicts aging should miss Patterson's *Stereotyping of the Elderly in Literature, Television and Films*,[7] sponsored by the Ohio State Commission on Aging. She has prepared two impressive units for high school classes, replete with suggestions for classroom activities and containing rich lists of novels, short stories, plays, and films in which she designates authors who do and do not stereotype older people. Among the adolescent novels she recommends as nonstereotypical are Schoen's *Place and Time*, Byar's *Trouble River*, Wagner's *J.T.*,

Schaefer's *Old Ramon*, Burgess' *The Small Woman*, Hooke's *The Starveling*, Wersba's *The Dream Watcher*, Sneve's *High Elk's Treasure*, and Brenner's *A Year in the Life of Rosie Bernard*.

For secondary-level students who are ready for adult reading, the literature is even more rich and varied. Old age may not figure prominently in 20th-century American writing, but the corpus of world literature since classical times offers students countless portrayals of old age from a wide variety of perspectives.[8] From Plato and Aristotle through Swift and Hardy to Hesse and Beckett, old age has had its full share of exposure. Many secondary students today can read and discuss with profit such novels as Achebe's *Things Fall Apart*, Balzac's *Pere Goriot*, Beckett's *Malone Dies*, Bellow's *Mr. Sammler's Planet*, Buck's *The Good Earth*, Cary's *The Horse's Mouth*, Gibson's *A Mass for the Dead*, Hemingway's *Old Man and the Sea*, Hilton's *Goodbye Mr. Chips*, Paton's *Cry the Beloved Country*, Spark's *Momento Mori*, Trollope's *The Warden*, and Updike's *The Poorhouse Fair*.

They can also gain insight into old age as well as enjoy such short stories as Babel's *Sunset and the End of the Almshouse*, Beckett's *The End*, Bellow's *Leaving the Yellow House*, Buck's *The Old Demon and the Old Mother*, Canfield's *Old Man Warner* and *Heyday of the Blood*, Cather's *Neighbor Rosicky*, Goodman's *A Cross Country Runner at 65*, Hawthorne's *Dr. Heidigger's Experiment*, O'Hara's *The Manager*, Singer's *The Old Man*, Steinbeck's *The Leader of the People*, Stuart's *Another April*, and Welty's *A Visit to Charity*.

Plays that depict aging sensitively for secondary students include Aiken's *Uncle Tom's Cabin*, Albee's *The American Dream*, Anouilh's *The Waltz of the Toreadors*, Beckett's *Endgame* and *Krapp's Last Tape*, Chekhov's *Uncle Vanya*, Hansberry's *A Raisin in the Sun*, Kaufman's *You Can't Take It With You*, Miller's *Death of a Salesman*, Moliere's *The Miser*, Osborne's *On Borrowed Time*, Shakespeare's *King Lear*, Shaw's *Back to Methuselah*, and Sophocles' *Oedipus at Colonus*.

Few English teachers will try to guide an entire class through a study of aging as it appears historically in American *belles lettres*, but the subject, or at least selected aspects of it, might serve admirably as a topic for individual or group projects. A student or a team of students might discover the reverence felt for age in Puritan times ("If any man is favored with long life, it is God that has lengthened his days."[9] and follow it in literature through the American Revolution to its disappearance. In novels and plays they might trace the change in our system of age relations which began late in the 18th century and which has culminated in our current adoration of youth. Students will probably be both amused and enlightened to find that pejorative terms for *old* (e.g., gaffer, fogey, codger, old goat, geezer) did not enter the language until the late 18th and early 19th centuries, reflecting the general loss of respect for the elderly in this period. When they study the Transcendentalists they can contrast the respect that Parker, Emerson, Longfellow, and Hawthorne felt for age with Thoreau's contempt: "Age is no better, hardly as well, qualified for an instructor as youth, for it has not profited so much as it has lost."[10] They can also appraise the accuracy and propriety of Whitman's raging against the indignities of old age in general and against the depredations, as he sees them, of his own later years in particular.

In a fascinating study high school classes will enjoy, cultural historian David Fischer finds that from about 1850 to 1950 "each successive spectrum shifted toward the left, toward an increasing antipathy for old age."[11] He makes a convincing case. When 20th-century authors choose to deal with old age, though they rarely do, Fischer finds that they do so with one of four motifs.[12] Least common is the theme in Hemingway's *Old Man and The Sea*, a story in which an old fisherman scores a bittersweet "triumph" over old age by bringing back to port at least the bare bones of the great fish he has hooked after 84 days of emptiness. The other three motifs are even less complimentary to age. One, represented by *The Grapes of Wrath*, shows old age to be not tragic—because tragedy entails nobility—but pathetic. When Rose-of-Sharon, who has just lost her baby, presses the lips of a starving old man to her breast, it is no act of human compassion; it only degrades them both. In Frost's poem, *Death of a Hired Man*, tired old Silas, unable to work or find shelter, comes "home" to die in a similarly pathetic scene. Another, at least equally demeaning theme, is what Fischer labels "the emptiness of old age"—exemplified by "Gerontion," a poem in which Eliot describes the grandfather matter-of-factly as "a dry brain in a dry season" and again as "an old man, a dull head among windy spaces." More devastating even than the emptiness motif, however, is the fourth and final theme, the utter absurdity not only of old age but also of all human life. Typifying this theme is the 69-year-old man in Beckett's one-act play *Krapp's Last Tape*, listening to his former self on tape and finding no satisfaction in it.

Fischer admires the Welsh poet Dylan Thomas for his refusal to bow to the ultimate sovereignty of age and death:

Do not go gentle into that good night
Old age should burn and rave at close of day
Rage, rage against the dying of the light.[13]

He says that American literature has nothing in it like Thomas' "spirited advice." This I regard as something of an overstatement. Gerontology's disengagement theorists certainly have their followers, but they also have a vigorous opposition, and American writers like Emerson, Holmes, Hemingway, Baldwin, Cather, Jewett, O'Connor, Sarton, Stegner, and Updike, among others, have all saluted old people who give age no quarter. In a gem of a novel, *As We Are Now*, Sarton paints a tragic but inspiring portrait of dear Miss Caro, "an old maid schoolteacher" who refuses to succumb to the sordid nursing home which imprisons and tries to break her. As she approaches the end, Miss Caro says:

I want my death to be something more like me than slow disintegration. "Do not go gentle into that good night" . . . the words so hackneyed by now, come back to me like a command from somewhere way down inside, where there is still fire, if only the fire of anger and disgust.[14]

And as a last goodbye, her friend Rev. Thornhill says:

You are a great person. . . . No, I mean it. Don't smile. I have seen in you what courage can be when there is no hope. I have seen the power of a human being to withstand the very worst and not be corrupted, and not change.[15]

In his zeal to defend the elderly, historian Fischer, I feel, turns polemicist and takes an unduly jaundiced view of 19th- and 20th-century American writers and their attitudes toward age. Not all of them have seen old age as pathetic, empty, or absurd. Old age in 19th- and 20th-century America has never been easy or joyous, and serious writers are unlikely to treat it as if it were. Where they have seen pathos and emptiness and absurdity in life's final stage, they have noted it, and where they have seen dignity and vigor and nobility, they also have marked it. In life and in literature, often the last years and the last days are neither heroic nor pathetic, neither ennobling nor empty. They often find old people facing their end with resignation, with some regret and some relief, still wondering what life in general, and theirs in particular, was for and about.

In *The Big Sky*, Guthrie's powerful and authentic novel on the opening of the West, the premier scout and Indian fighter, old Dick Summers, finally decides to retire to a farm in Missouri: "He could go back there and live and be happy, he reckoned, as happy as a hoss could be with the fire going out of him."[16] Finally ready to head back East, he listens to the wind and the mountains and the stars and hears their farewell:

> Goodbye, Dick Summers. . . . We'll see a sight of change but not you, Dick Summers. The years have fixed you. Time to go now. Time to give up. Time to sit back and remember. Time for a chair and a bed. Time to wait to die. Goodbye, Dick. Goodbye Old Man Summers.[17]

Life, he realizes, had been full of "rich doin's" but he wonders what he has to show for it in the end:

> It wasn't that he minded going under, it wasn't he was afraid to die and rot and forget and be forgotten; it was that things were lost to him more and more—the happy feeling, the strong doing, the fresh taste for things like drink and women and danger, the friends he had fought and funned with, the notion that each day would be better than the last, good as the last one was. A man's later life was all a long losing, of friends and fun and hope, until at last time took the mite that was left of him and so closed the score.[18]

One would be hard pressed to teach *The Big Sky* or *King Lear* or even *Nana Upstairs, Nana Downstairs* without "teaching" about old age, dying, and death. And why not? They are as vital and integral a part of literature as they are of life—and inescapable in both. The problem for English teachers then is not *whether* to teach about aging but *how*. First, how do teachers best prepare themselves psychologically as well as intellectually to deal with the subject? What do they read? What do they see and do? These are questions teachers must answer for themselves in view of their own life experiences. Second, how tactically is it best to handle aging in a literature class: to develop a structured unit on the subject or to deal with it strictly on an *ad hoc* basis only when it emerges from literature being read? This is a curricular decision individual teachers, departments, and schools had best make for themselves in view of their own special circumstances.

G.   Aging: A Cross-Cultural Perspective

Certainly there is some overlap in the problems that affect all aged, regardless of race or ethnicity. However, members of various minority groups may have different and perhaps unique concerns, and attention is now being directed toward just what these concerns are and how they can be solved.

Jill Quadagno

One of the most notable features of American education since World War II has been the move to globalize classroom instruction. In increasing numbers progressive teachers and curriculum builders are recognizing that an insular or ethnocentric curriculum is irrelevant and as self-defeating as an isolationist foreign policy. Others who are not so progressive have been forced by circumstances—by television and the Viet Nam War, by the explosion of our Hispanic population and the *Brown v. Board of Education* decision—to bring a multiethnic/international perspective into the classroom.

This was not always the case. Schools were once places from which most students emerged thinking that all Americans lived and thought, or at least *should* live and think, like WASPs. They also learned that intelligent and respectable people the world over either lived and thought like Americans, or at least *should* try to.

Today more and more students study the world as a system, and they emerge with some understanding of the interconnectedness and the interdependence of the world's peoples. They come to appreciate the Spaceship Earth concept, and they also come to see how that same concept applies to the mosaic of ethnic and racial groups that constitute the United States. They learn that the United States is both like and unlike other nations and can profit from becoming aware of both the similarities and the differences. They learn that members of different U.S. ethnic groups also have both commonalities and differences. They learn that *different* does not mean *better* or *worse* and that a recognition of difference can lead to a clearer understanding of one's self and one's own condition. It is learnings like these that the international/multicultural/cross-cultural educators stress.

One possible way to achieve these objectives and at the same time to better understand America and American aging is to study how other peoples of the world deal with the problem of age: to discover how the Russians and the Chinese, the Israelis, the Swedes, and the Zulus handle aging and also how within our own country Hispanics, Blacks, Jews, Italo-Americans, and Native Americans do the same.

Understanding how another society treats its elderly is one way of understanding that society's values and how it operates. And through contrastive analysis we come to better understand our own.

Depending both on the level of the students and on the class context in which they are considering age, a teacher may choose to survey a wide spectrum of cultures or to concentrate on a few representative types. It may serve a class's purpose to investigate aging in remote cultures like the long-lived Abkhasians of the Caucasus or the recently industrialized Japanese. On the other hand, in some schools it may be more meaningful to deal firsthand with cultures closer to home, with Blacks or Jews or Puerto Ricans. In any event students will have a chance to compare "us" with "them." They will have a chance to distinguish between what seem to be universal values and universal conditions of aging and what seem to be the products of particular kinds of cultural conditioning.

On the basis of their own experience as well as study, students can and should come up with their own categorization of what they judge to be generic aspects of aging and what they judge to be culture-bound aspects. Sociologists Donald Cowgill and Lowell Holmes[1] have drawn up just such a list, and secondary school students, again according to their degree of sophistication, might learn much by comparing their own list with it. Cowgill and Holmes maintain that the more modern a society is, the more insecure its elderly are and the lower their status is. In all the cultures they have studied they find eight "universals":

1. The elderly always constitute a minority.
2. Older females always outnumber older males.
3. Widows are a high proportion of the elderly.
4. All societies label some people old and expect them to behave that way.
5. As people age, they shift out of economic production into more sedentary advisory roles.
6. Some old people stay on as civic leaders.
7. Old people and their adult children feel responsibilities toward each other.
8. All people, including the old, value life and want it to last as long as possible.

In varying degrees, the authors say, all societies share these "universals."

On the other hand, Cowgill and Holmes find that the lot of the aged varies from society to society, not solely but largely as a reflection of the impact modernization has had on each society. On the strength of their research, the writers feel they can make several statements, all with a reasonable degree of assurance, about this variability. Some of the most significant are:

1. The more modernized a country, the older the age at which people are first regarded as "old."
2. The more modernized a society, the higher its proportion of older people.
3. The status the elderly occupy varies inversely with the proportion of the population they constitute.
4. The faster the rate of social change in a society, the lower the status of its elderly.
5. The greater the mobility of a population, the lower the status of the elderly.
6. The more urban or literate a society, the lower the status of its elderly.
7. The more useful a role the elderly perform, the higher their status.
8. An extended family arrangement tends to raise the status of the elderly.
9. In modernized societies, responsibility for care of the elderly shifts from the family to the state.
10. The Western emphasis on individualism and the role of work undermines the security and status of the elderly.[2]

Testing the validity of these propositions can be stimulating work for students. For example, here are just a few of the questions they might explore: What happens to the status of the elderly in highly modernized countries like Sweden and Denmark that are more welfare-minded than we and that provide totally free medical care, homemaker services, etc.? Do these countries exhibit less negative stereotyping of the elderly? In the Soviet Union does the vast pension system, combined with all the free public services, make the elderly independent and secure enough to retain the status level they attained in middle age? On the *kibbutz*, an institution dedicated to hard work, have the Israelis been able to invent less arduous roles for the aged that enable them to maintain their self-respect and status? These are tough and perhaps even unanswerable questions, but they are the kind that excite students and that can get them thinking about what it is and is not possible to do about improving our own aging situation.

Many students will begin their study of aging with extremely limited personal experience, their views on aging and the elderly shaped largely by a sensationalist press and media exposés. The grim picture some of them hold of what it means to grow old today in America will contrast sharply with other images they have of a idyllic aging either in "the old days" or in less developed societies. Their study should help eliminate these romantic stereotypes. Aging in preindustrial societies, particularly for people in the lower economic strata, they will discover, was usually harsh. They will learn that when life was a daily fight for survival, preindustrial societies often practiced a kind of "triage" in which the elderly were routinely done away with. In about half of the primitive tribes he studied, Leo Simmons[3] found that the aged were either neglected or abandoned. The Samoans used to bury their dead alive. In Siberia, Simone de Beauvoir reports, the Yakuts made beggars or slaves out of their old people in contrast to the Chukches who simply killed theirs in a great ceremonial feast.[4]

To students these practices may sound like barbaric behavior, but when they realize that the life, or at least the well-being, of the tribe itself often depended on its shedding of those who could make no contribution, they may have second thoughts. Our own approach to the elderly may seem somewhat less altruistic to students who conclude that we act as we do only because we can better afford to do so. In fact, some students may question how humane we actually are when we extend the lives of old people through medical technology, at times even against their will. Is it always a gift to keep an older person alive hooked up to a machine or stretched motionless on a nursing home bed? What does it profit a person to watch endless TV shows or to play endless bingo games? Students may come to question whether the greater longevity that modernization provides is actually a boon to the elderly when at the same time we deny them any useful role in life.

These situations pose moral dilemmas of the highest order, but they are dilemmas with which young people as well as adults not only can but should grapple. For example, under certain circumstances, are some lives worth more than others? If so, who makes the judgment? Under what conditions and to what extent are nonproducers (e.g., the elderly) entitled to society's care? Should care of the aged be primarily a family or a public responsibility? Obviously an elementary teacher would not handle issues such as these in the same way as a secondary teacher, but the students of both can and should come to grips with them, each at their own level.

Multicultural materials on aging are not yet plentiful, but teachers who wish to pursue a cross-cultural approach should at least look into the limited literature. A few mimeographed background papers may be particularly useful. One is a recent update on how European countries, including the Soviet bloc, treat their older people. In it Wilma Donahue, Director of the International Center for Social Gerontology, describes in some detail the evolution and current status of European health insurance systems, housing programs, and other organized support services for the aged.[5] Against this backdrop students will focus more sharply on our own efforts in these directions. Two other papers, both prepared for a 1979 conference sponsored by Global Perspectives in Education, may also be useful. One is Walter Beattie's *The Aging of Societies: Global Perspectives and Implications for Education*[6]. In it Beattie first traces aging trends (1970–2000) in both the developed and the developing worlds; he then outlines the impact these trends are now having and will have on political, economic, and educational institutions as well as on health and social services; and lastly he forecasts what implications the aging of the world's population has for the lives of particular individuals who are growing old.

In the second paper, *Global Perspective Education—Aging Education*[7], Robert Hanvey examines the current global education movement—its goals, practices, and prospects—and then speculates about what possible connections might be established between global education and aging education. He suggests that global and aging educators are both interested in questions of equity and fairness, that both try to create an awareness of wrong as a first step toward developing new attitudes and policies. Both, he says, believe that the schools should teach empathy and compassion, both are concerned with long-term demographic trends, both see the world and its problems in terms of "interdependence," and both have as goals clearer communication among people and the elimination of misperceptions and stereotypes. Each movement has its own radicals and its own conservatives, and while, to date, aging education has proved more tangible and personal, the goals and strategies of the two movements already appear to have enough in common to warrant their working together, at least occasionally, toward mutual ends.

Each of the working papers described above can be useful to the teacher of cross-cultural aging, but of most immediate practical value in the classroom is Gary Smith's *Teaching About Aging*, a document he prepared for the University of Denver's Center for Teaching International Relations. Smith has developed an impressive full-bodied unit for late elementary, junior high, and senior high students consisting of 18 teaching subsections, each designed to occupy one to four classroom hours. The subsections are carefully arranged to produce a cumulative effort, but teachers will find they also may be taught independently. The appendix contains 24 handouts which a teacher can duplicate to supplement each of the subsections being taught. Through a series of activities students first examine the preconceptions they hold about other peoples and the elderly. Then, through an examination of cross-cultural data, they learn that most behavior, including that toward aging, is not "natural" but rather the result of enculturation. The hoped-for result of the unit, which offers clearly defined cognitive, affective, and skill objectives for each subsection, is that students will reconceptualize and redefine their roles in relation to older people and the aging process. Given the imaginative quality of the unit's many exercises and the skill in its overall design, this is an outcome a teacher may actually expect to achieve.

6.   What Has Been Done? Recent Curricular Developments

Teachers at all levels encourage the idea that you have to talk about
things in order to understand them, because they wouldn't have jobs
otherwise. But it's phony, you know.

Denise Levertov

That aging education has taken so long to arrive on the educational
scene should not surprise us when we recognize that its parent discipline, gerontology, has itself only recently achieved academic respec-
tability. It was not until 1835 that Belgian scientist Lambert Quetelet
published what is usually considered the first substantial work in
gerontology, containing some impressive statistical research on intellectual and physical growth and decline.[1] Later in the 19th century
Sir Francis Galton studied the relationship between age and abilities
such as visual acuity and reaction time. After the turn of the century
biologists Charles Minot, Elie Metchnikoff, and Raymond Pearl also
made important contributions, but it was not until 1945 that the
Gerontological Society was founded, bearing witness to the number of
serious scholars by then dedicated to the field.

At the collegiate level, interest in gerontology first began to gain
real momentum after World War II. In just 20 years (1957–1976) the
number of institutions offering gerontology education leaped from 50
to over 600.[2] Today public and private, large and small, urban and
rural, two-year and four-year institutions, all are represented, some
offering an associate degree, others the bachelor's, master's, and more
than 60 the doctorate. This kind of growth is remarkable for a multidisciplinary field which is an upstart among the established academic
disciplines. In the early years that growth was encouraged because
gerontology attracted tuition-paying students, usually older ones, as
well as grant money at a time when both student enrollments and
funds were decreasing. In the future, however, as inflation and supply
side economic policies force more and more institutions into zero-

65

based budgeting, and as formerly generous federal allocations for human services begin to shrink, collegiate gerontology programs may be in for real trouble.

New as the field of gerontology is, even more recent is aging education. Until the 60's we find not a single documented reference to aging education as such at the precollege level. However, long before aging education—or even gerontology—was conceived, isolated elementary and secondary teachers certainly dealt with the concept of aging and the aged. In science some students studied senescence and physical decline; after reading *King Lear* and *Death of a Salesman*, some discussed the social and psychological aspects of growing old; in literature and social studies some learned how older people fare and have fared in other times and in other cultures; in American history or problems of democracy courses others studied our social security and medicare systems.

In elementary schools it is not new for a teacher to develop a unit on grandparents and in it to combine work in language arts, social studies, art, and science. Children have always read books like *Grandmother and I*, *The Giving Tree*, and *Matt's Grandfather*.[3] Even had they tried—and some may have—schools could not have excluded aging and age-related concerns from the classroom. Once life enters the school, so too, perforce, do aging, dying, and death. That age, aging, and the aged are topics in the American classroom, therefore, is not new. What is new is that they are consciously examined, that educational aims are being clarified and a body of instructional theory developed, and that materials and methods for accomplishing predetermined ends are being created and assembled.

Before turning to specific examples of current teaching, however, let us call attention to two valuable clearinghouses. The first is the U.S. Administration on Aging's National Clearinghouse on Aging, which operates the Service Center for Aging Information (SCAN). Modeled on the ERIC system, SCAN provides numerous services to the wider gerontological community: it collects and disseminates information on model projects, maintains a computerized data base for literature searches, supplies about 200 microfiche repositories located throughout the country, compiles bibliographies on special topics, and makes referrals to other appropriate sources of information.

The second agency, the Clearinghouse for Elementary and Secondary Aging Education (CESAE), is devoted to pedagogical concerns. It was launched with support from the Tennessee Commission on Aging at Tennessee Technological University, Box 5112, Cookeville, TN

38501 and is directed by Dr. John Myers. CESAE provides a communication network and resource center for precollege educators. Semiannually it publishes a newsletter which summarizes the state of the art in precollege aging education and reviews particularly effective curricular materials. (Dr. Myers provides a quick response to all inquiries about aging education, and the Clearinghouse serves as a lively forum for the exchange of ideas and information among members).

In 1971, the White House Conference on Aging lamented that it was "a rare occurrence" for aging to be incorporated in school curriculums.[4] It still is, but a few notable exceptions provide encouraging precedents.

Teachers should become familiar with Cameron's *Views of Aging: A Teachers' Guide,*[5] a 177-page monograph issued by the University of Michigan's Institute of Gerontology. Too broad-gauged, perhaps, in her effort to provide materials suitable for all levels, elementary through college, Cameron nevertheless supplies innumerable suggestions, most of them particularly appropriate for junior and senior high school classes. Not intended as a full course, *Views of Aging* can be incorporated as a unit into an ongoing course or can serve as a springboard from which a teacher can construct individualized units. Focusing on three major topics: "A Personal View of Aging," "An Environmental View of Aging," and "A Societal View of Aging," Cameron provides topics and references for further study with a wide variety of discussion questions, class activities, and homework assignments; she also suggests a wealth of resources, in print and other media, and concludes with a set of reproduced papers, probably more useful to teachers than students.

Another full-bodied work which anyone interested in teaching about aging should know is Saxe's *The Young Look at the Old: Curriculum Building in the Area of Aging,*[6] available through the Gerontology Education and Training Center at San Jose State University. Saxe has written a highly useful manual for people developing either elementary or secondary programs in aging. She suggests a spectrum of goals for such programs and describes the nature and advantages of cross-generational, cross-cultural, and interdisciplinary teaching approaches. In ingenious and practical ways she explains how to dovetail aging education with such areas as art, music, literature, social science, and physical education. She also has cogent suggestions to make about funding, staffing, and both pre- and in-service teacher training. Her appendices are useful, particularly the day-by-day lessons she outlines for grades 1–12 in three-week units. Indicative of the explicitly value-oriented thrust that permeates Saxe's work is Appendix G, entitled "Materials for Developing Positive Attitudes about Aging."

A more narrowly focused work is Smith's *Teaching About Aging*,[7] prepared at the University of Denver's Center for Teaching International Relations. The central aim of Smith's unit is to help students examine their preconceptions of other peoples, to recognize through exposure to cross-cultural information that most behavior is learned through enculturation, and to define or redefine their roles in relation to old people and the aging process. Smith gears the unit to grades 6–12; carefully articulates its cognitive, affective, and skill objectives; outlines 18 discrete classroom activities, in several of which U.S. attitudes toward aging are compared with those of other societies; and then provides master sheets for 24 classroom handouts. It should be a highly useful resource for the teacher who favors a cross- or multicultural approach, and may be used either in toto or eclectically.

Available unfortunately only on ERIC microfiche is Strubbe's "Aging in America: Fact, Fiction, and Feeling,"[8] a paper that she presented at the 1979 annual meeting of the National Council for the Social Studies. In it Strubbe outlines 13 secondary-level lessons on aging in America, each lesson to take one day and each complete with objectives, background information, reproducible student handouts, a list of materials needed, and evaluation forms. After examining their own beliefs and feelings about aging, students identify changing characteristics of the older population in the United States; study its diversity; settle on criteria for determining "oldness"; see growing old through popular song lyrics; discuss age-grading and the mass media's role in reinforcing age stereotypes; study housing, health, and other needs of older people; trace the role of work in American society and its relation to retirement; and probe possible means of improving the quality of life for older Americans. This highly informative, 107-page paper concludes with a short test and a list of teacher resources.

Though not of the same quality as the three documents just described, one ERIC paper sponsored by the Ohio State Commission on Aging, "Curricular Considerations for Elementary Schools: Death and the Aging Process" by Joan Jones and others,[9] with an annotated bibliography by Esther Jacobs, may also prove helpful. Its 21 pages provide under one tent a rationale for aging and death education at the elementary level; 12 broad goals to serve as guidelines for curriculum construction; 24 specific objectives; suggestions for in-service teacher education; six model elementary school lessons and one for the junior high school; and, lastly, an extensive list of annotated audio-visual and print resources.

More narrowly focused and more orthodox in form is a two- to three-week "activity unit" on the sociology of aging which Beverly Jo Croom prepared for her classes at North Clayton Senior High School (College Park, Georgia).[10] Stressing firsthand learning in the community, Croom requires her students to formulate testable hypotheses to which they then apply the process of scientific inquiry. Part I of the unit contains five well-outlined, predictably stimulating activities for all students and serves as an introduction to the study of aging; Part II consists of five slightly more intricate learning activities to be assigned to small groups; and Part III involves students in individual projects, which they work on from the outset of the unit and present to the class at its conclusion. Croom includes no evaluation plan and makes no claims for the unit's achieving its objectives, but the clarity of her conception and the imaginative quality of the activities she has devised suggest that under the direction of an informed teacher the unit would succeed with teen-agers at almost any level of academic competence.

Aimed at both elementary and secondary instruction is a *Handbook for Instruction in Aging*[11] which the California Department of Education has prepared to serve as a guide to help teachers and administrators develop curriculums on aging as part of their daily classroom activities. The booklet reflects the uneven quality of committee authorship, but it offers teachers new to the field an instructional framework they may find useful as a starting point. The handbook delineates five content areas of instruction: chronological aging, physiological/biological aging, sociocultural aspects of aging, psychological aging, and the community and the older individual. For each of these content areas the handbook articulates in grid format the goals, concepts, and objectives for elementary and then for secondary grades. Available also with the handbook is *Education About Aging: Bibliography and Resource List*,[12] a valuable 17-page listing, partially annotated, of age-related print and media materials.

Exclusively for elementary teachers, another valuable resource is *Activities for Teaching About Aging*,[13] 65 color-coded pages edited by H. Mason Atwood and prepared by K–6 teachers in Ball State University's Teacher Education Program on Aging. The activities, grade by grade, are categorized by subject area (language arts, mathematics, social studies, science and health, physical education, music, art, and general) as well as by aging topic (income, health, housing, education, nutrition, and retirement). This richly detailed work concludes with four ample appendices suggesting a wealth of further resources.

Three additional ERIC documents that deal explicitly with college-level courses nevertheless warrant the attention of elementary and secondary educators. Each course has its own unique flavor and something imaginative to suggest to precollege teachers. In "Organizing a Course in the Psychology of Aging,"[14] Beverly Gounard describes a lower-level undergraduate course she has taught at the State University of New York (Buffalo). Her use of simulation exercises, interviews, projective testing, field trips, and guest lectures may be particularly helpful. Nancy O'Connor has developed another unusual course especially for students unable to attend a congregate class.[15] She calls it *Teaching in the Boondocks: A Model for Independent Study of the Psychology of Aging.* O'Connor, too, makes extensive use of individualized activities, all of them imaginative and most of them promising for secondary students.

The third paper, "An Experimental English 1002 Course," describes Helen Naugle's advanced composition course at Georgia Institute of Technology.[16] Naugle has modeled her experimental section on the famous Foxfire Project. She spends the first two weeks working on composition skills, and then matches each student with an elderly resident at a "Golden Age" home. Students spend the next four weeks interviewing their elderly partners and writing papers growing out of their interviews. The remainder of the course then follows more conventional composition class procedures. Although its central goal is "improvement in style and mastery of the form and mechanics of writing," Naugle is convinced that the experimental course goes beyond its objectives and enhances student development in oral communication, creativity, ingenuity, and individual responsibility. Although students in the experimental section did not outperform other English 1002 sections on their final writing examination, their attitudes toward writing and their course experiences were vastly different. Unlike the regular control group students, they were enthusiastic about what they had done. One wrote: "You learned by doing things and by actual experience rather than just talking about it. I learned not only how to write better papers, but also how to talk to people and get them to talk about themselves." According to Naugle:

Perhaps the greatest humanistic quality of the course was the rapport built up between the aged and the youth. The students grew to respect, admire, almost love the withered, gnarled has-beens who have never made a million dollars—indeed, many of whom did not even speak standard English.[17]

It is interesting to note that not one of these college-level courses restricts itself to cognitive ends. Gounard talks about her desire "to foster positive attitudes toward aging and the aged." O'Connor seeks to "sensitize the student to an empathetic position of the aged." And rhetoric instructor Naugle takes more pride in the fact that her students learned "to bridge the generation gap," that "they related as mature young people on the job rather than as brow beaten students trying to make it in the System," than she does in their improved writing. To the extent that these examples are indicative, college courses in aging, no less than precollege ones, choose to include among their goals changing student attitudes, values, and even behavior.

Since aging educators must deal with the end-of-life cycle, they should familiarize themselves with at least some of the voluminous materials on death and dying as well as with the growing literature on teaching children and adolescents about the subject. Elementary teachers particularly will find rich stores of information and ideas in Grollman's *Explaining Death to Children*[18] and Mills' *Discussing Death*,[19] while those at both elementary and secondary levels may find helpful suggestions in my own *Death and Dying Education*.[20]

Books themselves, of course, are not the only source of help for those intent on building a curriculum in aging. Other resources are available at the many universities that have gerontology centers, notable among them the University of Southern California, the University of Michigan, and Syracuse University. At least 40 such institutions offer degrees in the field and many more offer courses and concentrations. Each state has its Office on Aging, normally in the capital city, and in Washington, D.C., one can contact the U.S. Administration on Aging (ADA) in the Department of Health and Human Services, as well as the National Council on the Aging, the Gerontological Society, the National Retired Teachers Association, and the American Association of Retired Persons, all of which publish regularly in the field. In addition, there are a number of journals which can be extremely helpful—for example, *The Gerontologist*, the *Journal of Gerontology*, *Aging*, *Omega*, and *Human Development*.

Outside the universities in-service training possibilities are also becoming available. One prime example is a federally funded three-year (1979–82) Title IV-C project—the Teaching and Learning About Aging (TLA) project—which social studies teacher Fran Pratt directs in the Acton–Boxborough (Mass.) Regional School District. The project's aim is to make K–12 teachers and students and the local communities more aware and understanding of age-related issues. In cooperation with the University of Lowell, Pratt first held an intensive two-week summer course and followed it immediately with a three-week workshop in which 18 teachers developed curriculum modules in a wide variety of grades and subject areas to pilot in 1979–80. The project reproduces those units that test well for the use of other interested teachers, continues to run its curriculum development workshop, maintains a fully equipped resource center, and provides teachers with a plentiful supply of aging materials and activities. The project also sponsors forums and programs of intergenerational contact between students and the elderly, publishes a newsletter, and works on outreach to surrounding communities. This kind of grass-roots project, funded at the local, state, or federal level and managed by an astute and knowledgeable local director, provides the most exciting as well as the most practical kind of in-service teacher training. At the same time it can stimulate entire communities to make the lives of older people more fulfilling. Hopefully, Pratt's project will be replicated many times throughout the country. Information and a complete list of publications are available from TLA Project, McCarthy-Towne School, Acton, Mass. 01720.[21]

7.   Aging Education and the Generation Gap

Strangely enough, the aged have a lot in common with youth; they
are largely unemployed, introspective and often depressed; their
bodies and psyches are in the process of change, and they are heavy
users of drugs. If they want to marry, their families tend to
disapprove. Both groups are obsessed with time.

Time, Aug. 3, 1970

In a fascinating study of the rise of student movements from
ancient to modern times and across Western and non-Western cultures, Feuer posits a set of universal themes which he sees manifest
themselves in every era. One of these themes, less studied and even
less understoood than class struggle, is *generational conflict*. To some
degree, in all times and in all places, Feuer says, difficult-to-define
emotions surge from unconscious depths in the young and drive them
to rebel against what they perceive as alienation and exploitation.
Each new generation, then, stages an emotional rebellion in which
"there is always present a disillusionment with and a rejection of the
values of the older generation" and a conviction that their generation
has a special historical mission to fulfill where the older generation,
other elites, and other classes have failed."[1]

This sense of repression and this urge to lash out can exist at a
societal level and also within the family. They become most acute,
naturally, when a social order or a family operates gerontocratical-
ly—that is, when older people by virtue of being old hold a disproportionate share of power and exert a disproportionate share of control. When these conditions prevail and when at the same time the
young judge that the old have failed in their responsibilities, youth is
most restive and most likely to rebel. On the strength of an impressive
collection of data on student movements, Feuer says:

The conflict of generations is a universal theme in history. Under
fortunate circumstances [the conflict] may be resolved within a
generational equilibrium. Under less happy circumstances, it

becomes bitter, unyielding, angry, violent; this is what takes place when the elder generation, through some presumable historical failure, has become de-authorized in the eyes of the young.[2]

Are these conditions that we now have with us? By few criteria, I believe, can we label America a gerontocracy, President Reagan and the Supreme Court notwithstanding. However, at least from an adolescent or a child's perspective, youth today is powerless, is utterly dependent on its elders. It is also the case that young people feel adults have made a mess of a world and often of their private lives. They have bequeathed a world of Watergate, Viet Nam, pollution, terrorism, inflation and unemployment, unbridled competition, and broken homes. As Feuer and others maintain, intergenerational conflict may be a timeless theme, but the current situation in America seems to be particularly volatile and calls for immediate correctives.

Just as one can describe a society in terms of social stratification, one can also describe it in terms of age stratification. People in America are ranked by age, and the different social roles they play as well as the rewards they get—e.g., money, power, and prestige—are all age-related. A kind of cohesiveness, a "we-ness vs. they-ness," similar to that which develops in socially stratified groups also emerges in our system of age stratification. Like blacks, ethnic minorities, the unemployed and women, both the young and the old are denied status and power in America, and each group develops a sense of identity and solidarity. Unlike the situation in other systems of stratification, however, group cleavages are somewhat mitigated by the fact that individuals and cohorts, as they age, keep moving up, through, and eventually out of the age structure.

In our social order the various stratifying systems tend to cut across one another and thereby defuse conflict. Sociologists, however, speculate as to what would happen if the deprived in several systems were able to coalesce. As Foner says, "If there is kinship in adversity, then no matter what the basis of their handicaps, there is always the possibility of these deprived strata uniting in common cause."[3]

Education today is obviously age-stratified. It is heavily concentrated in the early years and tends to ensure that the young remain close to their family base. What would happen, muses Foner, if this stratification were to break down and we were really to develop a system of lifelong education.[4] If people had the chance to acquire social and vocational credentials throughout their lifetimes, how

74

much would this cut into the advantages now held by young people born into the "right" families? How much would our class system open up if we were to engineer a radical change in our current practice of education age-grading?

Equally interesting is the question of what would happen if two major "have-not" age groups were to make common cause, if the young (children and adolescents) and the elderly were to unite and demand a greater share of rewards and prerogatives now held by the middle-aged. We know how strong a bond often develops between grandparents and grandchildren, a warm bond that contrasts sharply with the hostility so commonly felt between parents and children. It may be reasonable, then, to expect a growing affinity between two generations separated by a middle generation, which becomes a kind of common enemy of both.

This is, indeed, a possible scenario, but sociologist Leonard Cain, after he weighs the evidence for future coalition vs. conflict between the young and the old, comes down decisively on the side of conflict. As he sees it, "the conflict of the young and the old is between two dependent, unemployed groups, whose birthdays may average fifty years difference, not strongly knit by kinship considerations, struggling for financial and economic support from an intervening middle-aged group."[5] People in the middle generation(s) are increasingly finding themselves forced to support both their children and their aged parents. At the same time, on a societal level, especially as we move closer to zero population growth, because more and more people live to be old, proportionately fewer wage earners remain to support not only themselves but the generations that precede and follow them. In an inflationary period or a time of scarce resources, an entire society or a family may have to choose between supporting education for the young or for the old, between funding CETA or medicare. Two out of three American children today get inadequate medical care; on the other hand, 14 percent of our elderly are forced to live below the poverty level.[6] How do we balance these needs? Since young and old are both victims of age discrimination, Gray Panther leader Maggie Kuhn calls on them to unite. But the two groups, like minority cultures, each with its own values, goals, and life experience, vie with each other, in competition for whatever resources they can obtain. Whether a common victimization will overcome such strong, built-in differences and lead to a coalition, therefore, is problematical.

One thing is certain. The gap is sharper, more divisive, and more destructive than ever before in our history. Children, parents, and grandparents relate to each other less often and less well, view each other with less respect and more distrust, see each other in terms of stereotypes, and have little understanding of each other's aspirations, motives, feelings, and capabilities. So deep and so wide is the gap that many on both sides despair of its ever being bridged.

We do have a choice: we can adopt the stance that inexorable historical and technological developments can only exacerbate generational differences and conflict, and since we are powerless in the face of these developments, the better part of wisdom is to learn to live with them. Or we can take a less gloomy approach and believe that increasing generational divisiveness is not inherent in our future, that through intelligent social engineering, we can keep the gap from widening, and perhaps even help close it.

If we see education as an institution that influences as well as reflects social currents, we may also see it as a force significant enough to nudge society toward cross-generational understanding. But exactly where do the schools fit into this picture? What role can and should they play? By virtue of their very existence they contribute to a distinctive youth culture, but is it possible for them, through conscious effort, to mitigate these effects? Other questions also suggest themselves. Are we to accept as a given that generational cultures represent a social malaise? If the schools actually can exert some influence on bridging generational gaps, is it a cost effective use of their time and energies? Are programs that aim to close the gap necessarily at the expense of programs in basic skills development, or can the former actually enhance the latter? Will success at closing the generation gap make any easier the achievement of other school goals? These are questions to which there are no ready answers, but they are questions that must concern any educator who worries about how our society and its schools can cope with generational differences and the "problem" of aging.

Growing up in America, most of us would agree, is not easy today. Each stage—childhood, adolescence, young adulthood, middle age, and old age—provides its own particular difficulties. In addition, each transition from one stage to the next presents its own set of traumas as we find ourselves confronted by new and often conflicting demands. One result is that we have little time to enjoy, in turn, being children, adolescents, young adults, and then older adults. Some of these difficulties in transiting are internal and developmental, but others are societal in origin, exacerbated by the rapidity of social change.

Forty years ago Davis[7] and more recently Keniston[8] pointed out that the faster the rate of social change, the wider the gaps between generations and the more difficult life becomes for those of all ages. Evidence abounds that since the turn of the century, propelled by technology, social change has occurred at an unprecedented rate. As critical world events occur in breathtaking succession, even people who are biologically close in years acquire different characteristics and values, and form different sociological generations. Radically different sets of experience tend to magnify differences and breed conflict between generations and also to increase the difficulty in moving from one life stage to the next. Witness how from 1950 to 1970 we saw in rapid succession the arrival of at least four generations: the silent generation, the conservative generation, the beat generation, and the new left generation.

"Contemporaries are not merely people born in the same year," says Sigmund Neuman. "What identifies them as people of one generation is decided by their common experience, the same decisive influence, similar historical problems."[9] As a result of being shaped by a unique set of experiences, each generation of children marches through the age-stages and acquires its own body of knowledge, its own attitudes and values, and its own expectations of what later age-stages will be, or at least ought to be, for them.

Of course, it is easy to exaggerate and dramatize generational differences and the media have been all too ready to do so, a situation that has prompted a number of academic correctives.[10] It is also easy to think of generational differences and problems of aging as something new. They are not. Both Plato and Aristotle pointed to generational conflicts as the prime mover in political change. According to Plato, from youth's perspective temperance is "unmanliness" and modesty is "silliness." "Insolence [the young] term breeding and anarchy liberty . . . the master fears and flatters his scholars, and the scholars despise their masters and tutors."[11] Older generations, says Aristotle, see the young as incorrigible idealists, dogmatists, and extremists.[12]

It may be debatable whether communication across generations is any more difficult today than it was in Socrates' time or whether aging in America presents more or fewer difficulties than it does in other contemporary cultures. But it is hardly debatable that growing old today in America can present horrendous problems, for both the elderly and the yet to be elderly. Robert Butler's 1975 Pulitzer prize-winning book *Why Survive? Being Old in America*[13] shocks its readers first with its title and then with its contents. Some of that shock comes from the enormity of the situation he describes, but some of it stems from the readers' utter ignorance of the aging condition. In recent years Butler and others have done much to sharpen public awareness, but much still remains to be done. It is my conviction that schools can play a vital role in developing public awareness, and some are already beginning to do so through programs of aging education, the best of which feature intergenerational activities.

Such programs are being funded by public and private agencies at local, state, and national levels. Most prominent at the national level is ACTION's Foster Grandparents program, which pays low-income elderly to provide support, guidance, and instruction to handicapped children. "The greatest thing that happens," says its director Jack Kenyon, "is the formation of invisible bonds between the old people, who also have special needs, and the children. All of a sudden they are important in someone's lives. Both of them blossom. They fall in love."[14] Thirty states have added their own money to the program, and in some areas, like Allegheny County, Pa., the elderly serve not only as grandparents but also as paraprofessional social workers. In another ACTION program, the Retired Senior Volunteer Program (RSVP), older citizens provide services to people of all ages: they work in social welfare agencies, hospitals, nursing homes, and courts as well as in museums, day-care centers, and elementary and secondary schools.

Largest and probably most successful of the intergenerational programs initiated in the 1970's is the National Retired Teachers Association (NRTA) project, Youth Conferences with Older Americans. Secondary school students—either through groups such as the honor society, student council, or future homemakers or through an individual English, social studies, or health class—plan and stage a one-day conference with senior citizens to discuss age-related community problems. NRTA has provided thousands of useful handbooks and from coast to coast hundreds of stimulating conferences have been held. Many have triggered continuing intergenerational programs.

In 1974 the American Association of Retired Persons (AARP) began its Generation Alliance Program (GAP) in the Chicago area, and since then thousands of other AARP chapters have begun GAP groups, some to hold cross-generational discussions and others to work together on community projects. Other organizations that have worked with the GAP or that have started similar projects of their own are the 4-H Clubs, Girl Scouts, Campfire Girls, and Kiwanis. New York City's Older Adult Project (OAP) provides over 1,000 tutors to 200 city schools. In Los Angeles, Dedicated Older Volunteers in Educational Services (DOVES) enables 1,500 aides and tutors to work in 219 schools. Miami's Older Volunteers in Education (MOVE) not only provides tutors but also develops educational games and materials. In Winnetka, Ill., over 500 elderly volunteers still work as school aides and resource people in a program begun in 1967.

One can point to other model programs. In Ann Arbor's Teaching-Learning Community (T-LC), funded by the Michigan Department of Education, senior volunteers (aged 60–87) work in a wide variety of school situations, including an art program where they help develop children's creative and constructive thinking.[15] Students' responses have been almost unanimously positive, and the director of a local nursing home whose elderly residents served as volunteers says the program "saved the lives of some of our seniors who were literally giving up their spirit."[16]

In most of these programs the elderly come to the young and work in schools, homes, and day-care centers, but in some the young come to the elderly. For example, at the P.K. Yonge Laboratory School (University of Florida) 6- to 8-year-olds regularly visit their "adopted grandparents" in nursing homes, write them letters, and work with them at arts, crafts, and music. A study in 1974–75 to assess the project's impact reported that as compared with a control group of classmates, and presumably as a result of the experience, these children "more frequently had attitude changes in a positive direction toward elderly persons."[17] In Milwaukee, patients in the Family Hospital Nursing Home and children in the Family Hospital's Day Care Center regularly exchange visits and spend one day a week in each other's quarters. Here again the goal of the program is increasing "understanding, support and encouragement between the ages," and the results are encouraging.[18] In Edmonds, Wash., a center director first inventoried the skills and hobbies of interested senior citizens and then matched them with public school teachers' requests for classroom help. What developed was Seniors Offering Useful Resources for Children's Education (SOURCE), a project that provides elementary classrooms with a rich smorgasbord of resources and a warm grandperson presence.[19] A similar program, but one that reaches all the district's schools as well as many others nearby, is the Teaching and Learning About Aging[20] project in the regional school district of Acton-Boxborough, Mass.

One particularly ingenious experiment belongs to the Easton-Redding, Conn., School District. First, selected senior citizens are paired with seventh and eighth grade students who have psychosocial problems. The seniors then work with these students to create a set of educational devices that the adolescents later put to use when they tutor elementary school students. From the Director's Report,[21] it appears that Senior Tutors for Educational Progress (STEP) goes far toward achieving its objectives for all three of its age groups. Cognitive objectives consist of improvement in reading, math, and handwriting skills, and affective objectives include improvement in self-concept, classroom behavior, and home adjustment.

Another intriguing program is Project CLASP (Children Learning about Aging in a Structured Program), funded by ESEA Title IV-C and directed by John Pini for grades 4–8 in the Rockland, Mass., public schools. Specially trained CLASP teachers have constructed an impressive curriculum guide that describes over 150 classroom activities on aging that incorporate the teaching of basic skills, and that includes scope and sequence charts for both aging and basic skills.[22] The project provides for classroom visits by elders, a living history program, a regular radio show, in-service programs for teachers, and informational programs for community groups.

Of the multitude of programs which are springing up across the states, three others call for brief comment here because individually each is exemplary and distinctive, and together they give an idea of the limitless possibilities in intergenerational programming. First is a neatly packaged four-session Unit on Aging prepared by VISTA volunteer Ann Paranya for sociology and marriage and family classes at Lexington, Mass., High School.[23] Two of the classes considered most productive in the unit consisted of "rap sessions" with a group of invited senior citizens. Unit evaluations on the part of both students and seniors indicate not only that the sessions were enjoyable and informative but also that they helped the two groups develop a healthier respect for each other.

Second is Downington Intergenerational Groups (DIG). In the summer of 1978 in the little town of Downington, 35 miles west of Philadelphia, over 400 people, ranging in age from 10 to 81, enjoyed eight solid days of activities planned and promoted by Recreation Director Pam Emory. Youngsters (aged 10–13) and oldsters (aged 60–81) painted together, square-danced, played cards, fished, made quilts, pitched horseshoes, prepared and ate meals, played checkers, made candles, and flew kites. They learned *from* each other and *about* each other. According to Director Emory, "DIG proved that the generations can indeed mix, and the bogeyman GAP is just an illusion."[24]

The third is a small program in New York City which in 1973 brought together 6 emotionally disturbed children from the Henry Ittelson Center for Child Research and 15 residents of the Hebrew Home for the Aged. Each Wednesday morning for three hours the children, with their teacher, an art instructor, and at times a few volunteer students from Mount St. Vincent College, came to work in the Home's arts and crafts shop alongside the elderly residents, who were unaware of the children's emotional problems. Pairing began to take place over time as each child gravitated to the resident he or she felt most comfortable with. The old people taught skills they had already mastered and as a result developed greater self-esteem. The children in turn received not only instruction but also rare love, support, and encouragement. One child actually recognized how much they and their newly found old friends resembled each other: "We are stubborn, and so are they. We are self-centered and they are self-centered."[25] Another child confided to her older friend, "You know, Anna, I'm a problem child," and Mrs. Weiss nodded, "Well, who doesn't have problems?"[26] Comments like these reflect a degree of mutual understanding, respect, and affection between old and young that intergenerational programs in the schools can aim at and, hopefully, often achieve.

It may be some comfort to know that we are not the only Western nation to suffer from ageism and also to become aware of the damage age segregation causes. In England, for example, the Old People's Council is convinced that conditions under which the elderly will live 40 years from now depend directly on the degree and quality of involvement young people have today with older people. One can predict, says the Council, how people will care, or *not* care, for elderly parents by the attitudes they develop toward their own aging and toward old people they know as children and adolescents. The Council, therefore, encourages a wide variety of old–young activities including in-class teaching by elderly volunteers.[27]

All of us in America, of course, eventually pay dearly for our increasingly rigid system of age stratification. The old never get to know the young, and so mistrust them. The young miss out on their past, visualize no future, and dread both old age and death, knowing as little of one as of the other. In the process, they become uncomfortable with their own growing up and maturing. Psychologist Urie Bronfenbrenner describes the full gravity of the situation in *Two Worlds of Children*, a study in which he contrasts growing up in America and the Soviet Union:

> We cannot escape the conclusion that if the current trend persists, if the institutions of our society continue to remove parents, other adults, and older youth from active participation in the lives of children, and if the resulting vacuum is filled by the

age-segregated peer groups, we can anticipate increased alienation, indifference, antagonism, and violence on the part of the
younger generation in all segments of our society—middle-class
children as well as the disadvantaged.[28]

It would be brash to suggest that intergenerational programs in
American educational institutions by themselves might reverse the
current trend. On the other hand, for the schools not to make every
effort to do so would appear to be indefensible.

References

Chapter One—Aging: What's the Fuss All About?
1. U.S. Department of Health and Human Services. *Facts About Older Americans, 1979.* (HHS Pub. No. 80-20006.) Washington, D.C.: Government Printing Office, 1980.
2. Harris, Diana K., and Cole, William E. *Sociology of Aging.* Boston: Houghton Mifflin, 1980. pp. 24–25.

Chapter Two—What Do the Young Know of Aging?
1. Jantz, Richard K., and others. "Children's Attitude Toward the Elderly." *Social Education* 41(6): 518–23; October 1977.
2. de Beauvoir, Simone. *The Coming of Age.* New York: Putnam, 1973. p. 800.
3. McTavish, Donald G. "Perceptions of Old Age: Review of Research Methodologies." *Gerontologist* 11(4): 90–101; Winter 1971, Part II.
4. Bennett, Ruth. "Attitudes of the Young Toward the Old: A Review of Research." *Personnel and Guidance Journal* 55(3): 138; November 1976.
5. Butler, Robert N., and Lewis, Myrna I. *Aging and Mental Health: Positive Psychosocial Approaches.* St. Louis: C. V. Mosby, 1973.
6. Barron, Milton L. "Minority Group Characteristics of the Aged in American Society." *Journal of Gerontology* 8(4): 477–82; October 1953.
7. Kogan, Nathan, and Shelton, Florence. "Beliefs About 'Old People'." *Journal of Genetic Psychology* 100: 93–111; 1962.
8. Butler, Robert N. "Age-ism: Another Form of Bigotry." *Gerontologist* 9(4): 243–46; Winter 1969.
9. Harris, Louis, and Associates. *The Myth and Reality of Aging in America.* Washington, D.C.: National Council on Aging, 1975.
10. (a) Hickey, Tom; Hickey, Louise; and Kalish, Richard A. "Children's Perceptions of the Elderly." *Journal of Genetic Psychology* 112: 227–35; June 1968. (b) Thomas, Elizabeth, and Yamamoto, Kaoru. "Attitudes Toward Age: An Exploration of School-Age Children." *International Journal of Aging and Human Development* 6(2): 117–29; 1975. (c) Ivester, Connie, and King, Karl. "Attitude of Adolescents Toward the Aged." *Gerontologist* 17 (1): 85–89; February 1977.
11. Jantz, Richard K., and others. *op. cit.* p. 519.

12. *Ibid.*
13. Lorge, I.; Tuckman, J.; and Abrams, A. "Attitudes of Junior and Senior High School Students Toward Aging." *Growing with the Years*. Report of the New York State Joint Legislative Committee on Problems of the Aging. Albany: the Committee, 1954. p. 59–63.
14. Kastenbaum, Robert, and Durkee, Nancy. "Young People View Old Age." *New Thoughts on Old Age*. (Edited by Robert Kastenbaum.) New York: Springer, 1964. pp. 237–49.
15. Kogan, Nathan, and Shelton, Florence. *op. cit.*
16. Bell, Bill, and Stanfield, Gary G. "The Aging Stereotype in Experimental Perspective." *Gerontologist* 13(3): 341–45; Autumn 1973, Part I.
17. Amir, Yehuda. "Contact Hypothesis in Ethnic Relations." *Psychological Bulletin* 71(5): 319–42; May 1969.
18. Auerbach, Doris N., and Levenson, Richard L. "Second Impressions: Attitude Change in College Students Toward the Elderly." *Gerontologist* 17(4): 362–66; August 1977.
19. Kogan, Nathan. "Attitudes Toward Old People: The Development of a Scale and an Examination of Correlates." *Journal of Abnormal and Social Psychology* 62(1): 44–54; January 1961.

Chapter Three—Can Aging Be Taught?
1. Rosenfeld, Albert. "The New LSD: Life-Span Development." *Saturday Review*, October 1, 1977. pp. 32–33.
2. Mead, Margaret. "Grandparents as Educators." *Teachers College Record* 76(2): 244–45; December 1974.
3. Grambs, Jean. "Grow Old Along With Me . . . Teaching Adolescents About Age." *Social Education* 44(7): 595–98, 650; November–December 1980.

Chapter Five—Aging: What Is There To Learn and Teach?
A. The Biology of Aging
1. Shock, Nathan W. "Biological Theories of Aging." *Handbook of the Psychology of Aging*. (Edited by James E. Birren and K. Warner Schaic.) New York: Van Nostrand Reinhold, 1977. pp. 103–13.
2. Shore, Herbert. "Designing a Training Program for Understanding Sensory Losses in Aging." *Gerontologist* 16(2): 157-65; April 1976.

B. The Psychology of Aging
1. Wechsler, David. *The Measurement and Appraisal of Adult Intelligence*. (Edited by Diana S. Woodruff and James E. Birren.) Baltimore: Williams and Wilkins, 1958.
2. Schaic, K. Warner. "Age Changes in Adult Intelligence." *Aging: Scientific Perspectives and Social Issues*. (Edited by Diana Woodruff and James E. Birren.) New York: D. Van Nostrand, 1975. pp. 111–24.
3. Boswell, James. *Life of Johnson*. (Edited by L.F. Powell.) Oxford: Clarendon Press, 1934. Vol. 4, p. 181.
4. (a) Riley, Matilda, and Foner, Anne. *An Inventory of Research Findings: Aging and Society*. New York: Russell Sage, 1968. Vol. 1. (b) Welford,

A.T. "Motor Performance." *Handbook of the Psychology of Aging.* (Edited by James Birren and K. Warner Schaic.) New York: Van Nostrand Reinhold, 1977. pp. 450–96. (c) Sheppard, Harold. "Work and Retirement." *Handbook of Aging and the Social Sciences.* (Edited by Robert Binstock and Ethel Shanas.) New York: Van Nostrand Reinhold, 1976. pp. 2 and 6–309.

5. Riley, Matilda, and Foner, Anne. *op. cit.*
6. Dennis, Wayne. "Creative Productivity Between the Ages of 20 and 80 Years." *Journal of Gerontology* 21(1): 1–8; January 1966.
7. Bock, E. Wilbur. "Aging and Suicide: The Significance of Marital Kinship, and Alternative Relationships." *Family Coordinator* 21 (1): 71–79; January 1972.
8. U.S. Public Health Service. *Vital Statistics of the United States, 1970. Vol II: Mortality, Part A.* Washington, D.C.: National Center for Health Statistics, U.S. Government Printing Office, 1970. pp. 24–25.
9. Pfeiffer, Eric. "Psychopathology and Social Pathology." *Handbook of the Psychology of Aging.* (Edited by James E. Birren and K. Warner Schaic.) New York: Van Nostrand Reinhold, 1977. p. 656.
10. Frankfather, Dwight. *The Aged in the Community.* New York: Praeger, 1977. p. 132.
11. Butler, Robert N., and Lewis, Mynra I. *Aging and Mental Health: Positive Psychosocial Approaches.* St. Louis: C.V. Mosby, 1973.
12. Reichard, Suzanne; Livson, Florine; and Peterson, Paul. *Aging and Personality.* New York: John Wiley, 1962. pp. 170–72.
13. Butler, Robert N., and Lewis, Myrna I. *op. cit.* p. 50.

C. Aging: The View from History
1. Fischer, David A. *Growing Old in America.* New York: Oxford University Press, 1977. pp. 6–10.
2. *Ibid.* p. 19.
3. *Ibid.* p. 79.
4. *Ibid.* p. 78.

D. The Politics and Economics of Aging
1. Laswell, Harold D. *Politics: Who Gets What, When and How.* New York: McGraw-Hill, 1936.
2. Brotman, Herman B. "Voter Participation in November 1976." *Gerontologist* 17(2): 157–59; April 1977.
3. Norval, Glenn, and Grimes, Michael. "Aging, Voting and Political Interest." *American Sociological Review* 33(4): 572; August 1968.
4. Bacon, Francis. "Of Youth and Age." *Essays.* Mount Vernon, N.Y.: Peter Pauper Press, no date. p. 166.
5. Binstock, Robert H. "Interest Group Liberalism and the Politics of Aging." *Gerontologist* 12(3): 265–80; Autumn 1972.
6. Cutler, Neal, and Schmidheuser, John. "Age and Political Behavior." *Aging: Scientific Perspectives and Social Issues.* (Edited by Diana Woodruff and James E. Birren.) New York: D. Van Nostrand, 1975.
7. Hudson, Robert B., and Binstock, Robert H. "Political Systems and Aging." *Handbook of Aging and the Social Sciences.* (Edited by Robert

H. Binstock and Ethel Shanas.) New York: Van Nostrand Reinhold, 1976. pp. 369–70.

8. Glenn, Norval D. "Aging and Conservatism." *Annals of the American Academy of Political and Social Science* 415: 176–86; September 1974.

9. Butler, Robert N. *Why Survive? Being Old in America.* New York: Harper & Row, 1975. pp. 334–43.

10. *Ibid.* p. 341.

11. Jacobs, Ruth H., and Hess, Beth B. "Panther Power: Symbol and Substance." *Aging, The Individual and Society.* (Edited by Jill S. Quadagno.) New York: St. Martin's, 1980. p. 413.

12. U.S. Bureau of the Census. *Current Population Reports.* Special Studies Series P-23, No. 59. Washington, D.C.: Government Printing Office, 1976. p. 51.

13. Kreps, Juanita M. "Intergenerational Transfers and the Bureaucracy." *Aging, the Individual and Society.* (Edited by Jill S. Quadagno.) New York: St. Martin's, 1980. pp. 440–54.

E. Aging: A Sociological Perspective

1. Harris, Louis, and Associates. *The Myth and Reality of Aging in America.* Washington, D.C.: National Council on Aging, 1975.

2. Hochschild, Arlie. *The Unexpected Community.* Englewood Cliffs, N.J.: Prentice-Hall, 1973.

3. Auerbach, Doris N., and Levenson, Richard L. "Second Impressions: Attitude Change in College Students Toward the Elderly." *Gerontologist* 17(4): 362–66; August 1977.

4. Sheehy, Gail. *Passages: Predictable Crises of Adult Life.* New York: Dutton, 1976.

5. Burgess, Ernest W. *Aging in Western Societies.* Chicago: University of Chicago Press, 1960. p. 20.

6. Cumming, Elaine, and Henry, William E. *Growing Old.* New York: Basic Books, 1961. p. 161.

7. Havighurst, Robert J.; Neugarten, Bernice L.; and Tobin, Sheldon S. "Disengagement and Patterns of Aging." *Middle Age and Aging.* (Edited by Bernice L. Neugarten.) Chicago: University of Chicago Press, 1968. p. 132.

8. Tibbitts, Clark. "Some Social Aspects of Gerontology." *Gerontologist* 8(2): 131–34; Summer 1968.

9. Goode, William J. *World Revolution and Family Patterns.* New York: Free Press of Glencoe, 1963. p. 7.

10. Shanas, Ethel, and others. *Old People in Three Industrial Societies.* New York: Atherton, 1968. pp. 192–96.

11. Neugarten, Bernice L., and Weinstein, Karol K. "The Changing American Grandparent." *Middle Age and Aging.* (Edited by Bernice L. Neugarten.) Chicago: University of Chicago Press, 1968. pp. 280–85.

12. (a) Klemach, David L., and Ruff, Lucinda L. "Appropriateness of Heterosexual Alternatives to Marriage for Older Persons." *Alternative Lifestyles* 3(2): 137–49; May 1980. (b) Drexel, Paula L., and Arant, W. Ray. "Neogamy and Older Persons: An Examination of Alternatives for Inti-

macy in the Later Years." *Alternative Lifestyles* 1(1): 13–72; February 1978. (c) Streib, Gordon F. "An Alternative Family Form for Older Persons: Need and Social Context." *Family Coordinator* 27(4): 413–20; October 1978. (d) Streib, Gordon F., and Hilker, Mary A. "The Cooperative 'Family' as an Alternative Lifestyle for the Elderly." *Alternative Lifestyles* 3(2): 167–85; May 1980. (e) Nass, Gilbert D.; Libby, Roger W.; and Fisher, Mary P. *Sexual Choices.* Belmont, Calif.: Wadsworth, 1981. pp. 313–41.

F. Literature and Aging
1. Barnum, Phyllis W. "The Aged in Young Children's Literature." *Language Arts* 54(1): 29–32; January 1977.
2. *Ibid.* p. 32.
3. Constant, Helen. "The Image of Grandparents in Children's Literature." *Language Arts* 54(1): 33–40; January 1977.
4. Seefeldt, Carol, and others. "The Coming of Age in Children's Literature." *Childhood Education* 54(3): 123–24; January 1978.
5. Peterson, David A., and Karnes, Elizabeth L. "Older People in Adolescent Literature." *Gerontologist* 16(3): 225–31; June 1976.
6. *Ibid.* p. 230.
7. Patterson, Joyce. *Stereotyping of the Elderly in Literature, Television and Films.* ED 163 343. 1975. (microfilm.)
8. Myers, John. *Characterization of the Aged in Literature.* ED 163 347. 1974. (microfilm.) p. 8.
9. Mather, Increase. *Dignity and Duty of Aged Servants.* p. 52. As quoted in Fischer, David H. *Growing Old in America.* New York: Oxford University Press, 1977. p. 33.
10. Thoreau, Henry, *Walden.* New York: Modern Library, 1937.
11. *Ibid.*, pp. 122–35.
12. Fischer, David H. *Growing Old in America.* New York: Oxford University Press, 1977. p. 127.
13. Thomas, Dylan. "Do Not Go Gentle into that Good Night." *Collected Poems.* (Edited by Daniel Jones.) New York: New Directions, 1939. pp. 128–29.
14. Sarton, May. *As We Are Now.* New York: Norton, 1973. p. 121.
15. *Ibid.* p. 131.
16. Guthrie, A.B. *The Big Sky.* New York: Pocket Books (Cardinal edition), 1952. p. 219.
17. *Ibid.* p. 238.
18. *Ibid.* p. 239.

G. Aging: A Cross-Cultural Perspective
1. Cowgill, Donald O., and Holmes, Lloyd D., eds. *Aging and Modernization.* New York: Appleton Century Crofts, 1972.
2. *Ibid.* pp. 321–22.
3. Simmons, Leo W. *The Role of the Aged in Primitive Society.* New Haven: Yale University Press, 1945.
4. de Beauvoir, Simone. *Old Age.* London: Deutch Ltd., 1972. pp. 45–46, 51.

5. Donahue, Wilma T. *How Other Countries Treat Their Older People.* Washington, D.C.: International Center for Social Gerontology, no date. 63 pp. (mimeo.)
6. Beattie, Walter M. *The Aging of Societies: Global Perspectives and Implications for Education.* Syracuse: Syracuse University Gerontology Center, 1979. (mimeo.)
7. Hanvey, Robert G. "Global Perspectives Education—Aging Education." Paper prepared for Conference on Global Aging Trends and Education sponsored by Global Perspectives in Education, Inc. at Straus House, Catskill Forest Preserve, N.Y., August 23–26, 1979.
8. Smith, Gary R. *Teaching About Aging.* Denver: Center for Teaching International Relations, University of Denver, 1978.

Chapter Six—What Has Been Done? Recent Curricular Developments
1. Harris, Diana K., and Cole, William E. *Sociology of Aging.* Boston: Houghton Mifflin, 1980. p. 7.
2. Bolton, Christopher R., and others. *Gerontology Education in the U.S.: A Research Report.* Omaha: University of Nebraska Gerontology Program, 1978. pp. 55–65.
3. (a) Buckley, Helen E. *Grandmother and I.* New York: Lathrop, Lee and Shepard, 1962. (b) Silverstein, Shel. *The Giving Tree.* New York: Harper and Row, 1964. (c) Lundgren, Max. *Matt's Grandfather.* New York: Putnam, 1972.
4. *Training Background*, White House Conference on Aging, Washington, D.C., 1971. p. d.
5. Cameron, Marcia J. *Views of Aging: A Teaching Guide.* Ann Arbor: Institute of Gerontology, University of Michigan, 1978.
6. Saxe, Adele R. *The Young Look at the Old: Curriculum Building in the Area of Aging.* ED 166 071, 50 011 193. San Jose: San Jose State University, 1977.
7. Smith, Gary R. *Teaching About Aging.* Denver: Center for Teaching International Relations, University of Denver, 1978. (Also in ED 120 264, 50 009 379. 1975.)
8. Strubbe, Mary. *Aging in Ameria: Fact, Fiction, and Feeling.* ED 186 292, SC 012 279. 1979.
9. Jones, Joan, and others. *Curricular Considerations for Elementary Schools: Death and the Aging Process.* ED 163 349, CG 013 043. 1975.
10. Croom, Beverly Jo. "Aging Education for the High School Student." *Social Education* 42(5): 406–408; May 1978.
11. *Handbook for Instruction on Aging.* Sacramento: California State Department of Education, 1978.
12. *Education About Aging: Bibliography and Resource List.* Sacramento: California State Department of Education, 1977.
13. Atwood, H. Mason, ed. *Activities for Teaching About Aging.* Muncie, Ind.: Teacher Education Program on Aging, Ball State University, 1975.
14. Gounard, Beverly R. *Organizing a Course in the Psychology of Aging.* ED 157 457, HE 010 294. 1978.
15. O'Connor, Nancy. *Teaching in the Boondocks: A Model for Indepen-*

dent Study of the Psychology of Aging. ED 141 724, CG 011 567.
1976.

16. Naugle, Helen H. *An Experimental English 1002 Course.* ED 140 329,
CS 203 463. 1976.

17. *Ibid.* p. 17.

18. Grollman, Earl. *Explaining Death to Children.* Boston: Beacon Press,
1967.

19. Mills, Gretchen, and others, eds. *Discussing Death.* Homewood, Ill.: ETL
Publications, 1976.

20. Ulin, Richard O. *Death and Dying Education.* Washington, D.C.:
National Education Association, 1977.

21. (a) Dodson, Anita, and Hause, Judith. *Ageism in Literature: An Analysis
Kit for Teachers and Librarians.* Acton, Mass.: TLA Project, 1981. (b)
Dodson, Anita, and Hause, Judith. *Realistic Portrayal of Aging: A
Selected Annotated Bibliography.* Acton, Mass.: TLA Project, 1981. (c)
Frost, George. *Confrontation: Aging in America.* Acton, Mass.: TLA
Project, 1981. (d) Betourney, William. *Demographics of Aging: Implica-
tions for the Future.* Acton, Mass.: TLA Project, 1981.

Chapter Seven—Aging Education and the Generation Gap

1. Feuer, Lewis. *The Conflict of Generations.* New York: Basic Books,
1969. p. 11.

2. *Ibid.* pp. 527–28.

3. Foner, Anne. "Age in Society: Structure and Change." *Age in Society.*
(Edited by Anne Foner.) Beverly Hills: Sage Publications, 1975. p. 30.

4. *Ibid.* p. 31.

5. Cain, Leonard D. "The Young and the Old: Coalition or Conflict
Ahead?" *Age in Society.* (Edited by Anne Foner.) Beverly Hills: Sage
Publications, 1975. p. 41.

6. (a) Butler, Robert N. *Why Survive? Being Old in America.* New York:
Harper & Row, 1975. pp. xii, 5. (b) U.S. Department of Health and
Human Services. *Facts About Older Americans: 1979.* (HHS Pub. No.
80-20006.) Washington, D.C.: Government Printing Office, 1980.

7. Davis, Kingsley. "The Sociology of Parent–Youth Conflict." *American
Sociological Review* 5(4): 523–36; August 1940.

8. Keniston, Kenneth. *The Uncommitted: Alienated Youth in American
Society.* New York: Dell, 1960.

9. Neumann, Sigmund. "The Conflict of Generations in Contemporary
Europe." *Vital Speeches of the Day,* V: 623–28; 1939. Cited in Feuer,
Lewis. *The Conflict of Generations.* p. 28.

10. Conger, John J. "A World They Never Knew: The Family in Social
Change." *Youth and Culture: A Human Development Approach.* (Edited by
Hazel   B.   Kraemer.)   Monterey,   Calif.:
Brooks/Cole, 1974. pp. 407–26.

11. Feuer, Lewis. *op. cit.* p. 28.

12. *Rhetoric of Aristotle.* Cited in Kiell, Norman. *The Universal Experience
of Adolescence.* Boston: Beacon Press, 1964.

13. Butler, Robert N. *Why Survive? Being Old in America.* New York:
Harper & Row, 1975.

14. *Denver Post,* Feb. 4, 1981. p. 10.

15. Mehta, Margaret. "Charting the Grandperson Galaxy." *Phi Delta Kappan* 58(3): 244–47; November 1976.
16. Doyle, James R. "Digging for Human Treasure." *Educational Leadership* 34(1): 26–30; October 1976.
17. Whitley, Esstoya, and others. *From Time to Time: A Record of Young Children's Relationships with Aged.* Research Monograph No. 17, ED 128 088. 1976. p. 88.
18. Mitchell, Adelia, and Schachel, Chrystal. "Journey in Time: A Foster Grandparent Program." *Young Children* 34(3): 30–32; March 1979.
19. Strachan, Margaret P. "Teachers Are Getting Much Needed Help and Children Have a New Image of Grandma and Grandpa." *Instructor* 82(4): 1975; February 1973.
20. Pratt, Fran. *Teaching and Learning About Aging Newsletters.* Acton, Mass: Teaching and Learning About Aging Project, McCarthy-Towne School, 1979–80.
21. Pica, Teresa. *Project S.T.E.P.: Senior Tutors for Educational Progress.* ED 120 96, UD 015 825. 1975.
22. Pini, John, ed. *Aging Education: Project Clasp Curriculum Guide.* Rockland, Mass.: Rockland Public Schools, 1981.
23. Paranya, Ann C. *Unit on Aging.* ED 098 125, SO 007 913. 1974.
24. Emory, Pam. "A Program That Moves Older with Younger." *Parks and Recreation* 14(2): 16–19, 51; February 1979.
25. Streitfield, Elaine. "Young and Old Together." *Social Policy* 7(2): 100–102; November-December, 1976.
26. *Ibid.* p. 100.
27. National Old People's Welfare Council. *Annual Report for the Year Ending March 31, 1966.* London: British Information Services, 1966.
28. Bronfenbrenner, Urie. *Two Worlds of Children: U.S. and U.S.S.R.* New York: Russell Sage Foundation, 1970. pp. 116–17.